BUSINESS MENTORSHIP

Climbing the Success Ladder By Taking The Steps Of Those Who Have Gone Ahead Of You

BY STEPHEN AKINTAYO

Contents

INTRODUCTION
Business
Mentorship

A *mentor* is an individual with expertise who can help develop the career/business or life of a mentee. A mentor often has two primary functions for the mentee. The career/life-related function establishes the mentor as a coach who provides advice to enhance the mentee's professional performance and development. The psychosocial function establishes the mentor as a role model and support system for the mentee. Both functions provide explicit and implicit lessons related to professional development as well as general work–life balance.

For the purposes of this book, it is important to differentiate between the terms *protégé* and *mentee*. The term protégé has a clear history in mentoring research and applies to individuals who are sponsored, promoted by someone more experienced and influential. Usually, a protégé is chosen by their mentors and they tend to have a long-term relationship which entails working close together. Whereas, a mentee is guided by a mentor, who is more experienced. The mentee has the role of "learner" while the mentor simply offers advice but is not obliged to sponsor or promote them.

For instance, a mentee who needs business mentorship can have a mentor who is a serial entrepreneur or established retailer while the mentee themselves are building a food business. Although the fields are different, the mentee can learn from the business acumen of the mentor. But an upcoming hip hop artiste who is a protégé to a popular hip hop star will tend to dress like the latter, perform alongside them, go to events with them and even have access to their private lives.

Research has consistently found mentored individuals to be more satisfied and committed to their professions than non-mentored individuals (Wanberg, Welsh, & Hezlett, 2003). Furthermore, mentored individuals often earn higher performance evaluations, higher salaries, and faster career progress than non-mentored individuals. Mentors can also benefit from a successful mentoring relationship by deriving satisfaction from helping to develop the next generation of leaders, feeling rejuvenated in their own career development, learning how to use new technologies, or becoming aware of issues, methods, or perspectives that are important to their field.

In summary, mentorship is a relationship in which a more experienced or more knowledgeable person helps to guide a less experienced or less knowledgeable person

.

ABOUT THE AUTHOR

Stephen Akintayo, is an inspirational speaker and Serial Entrepreneur. He is the Chief Executive Officer of Stephen Akintayo Consulting International and Gtext Media and Investment Limited, a leading firm in Nigeria whose services span from digital marketing, website design, bulk sms, online advertising, Media, e-commerce, real estate, Consulting and a host of other services.

He was born in Gonge Area of Maiduguri, Borno State in a very impoverished environment and with a civil Servant as a Mother who raised him and his four other siblings with her meagre salary since his father's Contract Business had crumbled. His humble beginnings contributed to his philanthropic passion.

In his words; "Poverty was my surname. Hunger was my biggest challenge as a young boy. I had to scavenge through Elementary school to eat lunch. I didn't have lunch packs like other kids because we couldn't afford it. Things picked up in high school. Albeit, my mother still had to borrow money from her colleague to keep me in school each term. It was humiliating seeing their disdainful looks at my mum because of our constant begging. It hurt dearly. I hate Poverty and I strive to help more families come out of it".

Stephen Akintayo story is indeed a grass to grace one. It however saddens his heart that his hard-working mother died few years back due to ovarian cancer and never lived to see his successful endeavors and how much of a blessing he is to others.

Stephen, Also Founded GileadBalm Group Services which has assisted a number of businesses in Nigeria to move to enviable levels by helping them reach their clients through its enormous nationwide data base of real phone numbers and email addresses. It has hundreds of organizations as its clients including multinational companies like Guaranty Trust Bank, PZ Cussons, MTN, Chivita, among others.

He is also the Founder and President of two indigenous non-governmental organizations, *Infinity Foundation and Stephen Akintayo Foundation.* Infinity Foundation assists orphans and vulnerable children as well as mentor young minds. The foundation has assisted over 2,000 orphans and vulnerable children. It has also partnered with 22 orphanage homes in the country. In December 2015, Infinity Foundation launched Mercy Orphanage to care for victims and IDP's as a result of Boko Haram attacks in the Northern part of Nigeria.

The *Stephen Akintayo Foundation* gives out Financial Grants with 10 million Naira disbursed to 20 entrepreneurs during the pilot phase in 2015 and plans to grow that amount to 500 million naira annually by 2019. Other projects the foundation is involved in includes the *Upgrade Conference* and *The Serial Entrepreneur Conference* with thousands of attendees. The conferences are targeted at providing young entrepreneurs, career professionals an opportunity to learn and connect with excellent speakers, consultants and industry experts.

Also, the founder of *Omonaija,* an online radio station in Lagos currently streaming for 24 hours daily with the capacity to reach every country of the world. As founder and Director of *Digital Marketing School Nigeria*, Africa's leading digital marketing school, he is changing the approach to digital marketing training with a very robust training curriculum. The school issues diploma certificates in Digital Maketing, Tele Marketing and Neuro Marketing.

Stephen is a media personality in the Television, Radio and Print media. He anchors a programme on Radio Continental, tagged CEO Mentorship with Stephen Akintayo in addition to weekly column in some of Nigeria's national papers, including The Nation Newspaper and The Union Newspapers. He is also a social media guru.

His mentorship platform has helped thousands of people including graduates and undergraduates in the area of business as well as in building relationships. Stephen strongly believes young Nigerians with the passion for entrepreneurship can cause a business revolution in Nigeria and the world at large. He is a prolific writer and published author of several books including *Turning Your Mess To Message, Soul Mate, Survival Instincts* and *Mobile Millionaire.*

A member of *The Institute of Strategic Management*, Stephen obtained his first degree in Microbiology from *Olabisi Onabanjo University.* He is a trained Digital Marketing Consultant by the *Digital Marketing Institute* at *Harvard University,* a trained coach by *The Coaching Academy UK* and he has several other professional trainings inside and outside Nigeria. Currently, he is running a Masters In Digital Marketing and MBA in Netherlands.

He is also an ordained Pastor with *Living Faith Church Worldwide* and is happily married and blessed with two sons; Divine Surprises and Future.

To invite Stephen Akintayo for a speaking engagement kindly email: info@stephenakintayo.com or call: 08180000618.

CHAPTER ONE
MENTORSHIP

"Mentoring is to support and encourage people to manage their own learning in order that they may maximize their potential, develop their skills, improve their performance and become the person they want to be." Eric Pasloe

In my work as a finance and business coach, I realized that there are several helpful resources and lifelines that very few people take advantage of. And mentorship is one of such resources. It is such a sad reality because mentorship is one of the resources that do not have to cost you an arm and a leg. Having a mentor can elevate your professional capabilities exponentially.

And by the way, mentors can be amazing people. If you take the time to develop a strong mentorship relationship, not only do you get access to a wealth of knowledge and experience, but you might also end up with a lifelong friend and potential future business partner. In fact, I sometimes see no downsides to it, as you get to learn from the strengths and weaknesses of your mentor. The roots of the mentorship dates way back to ancient times as the word itself was inspired by the character of *Mentor* in *Homer's Odyssey*.

Mentorship

Of course, if you aren't familiar with the concept, you may have questions about how it all works. So, what exactly is mentorship? Mentorship is a relationship in which a more experienced or more knowledgeable person helps to

guide a less experienced or less knowledgeable person. The mentor may be older or younger than the person being mentored, but he or she typically has a certain area of expertise. It involves a learning and development partnership between someone with vast experience and someone who wants to learn.

Mentorship experience and relationship structure can significantly affect the amount of psychosocial support, career guidance, role modeling, and communication that occurs in the mentoring relationships in which the protégés and mentors engaged.
The person in receipt of mentorship may be referred to as a ***protégé*** or ***protégée***, an apprentice or, in the 2000s, a **mentee**.

"Leaders... should influence others... in such a way that it builds up, encourages and edifies them so they can duplicate this attitude in others"

Bob Goshen

Mentoring which is the process of mentorship involves communication and it is relationship-based, but its precise definition can be a little elusive with so many different definitions. However, I would define mentoring as a process for increased social capital, the informal transmission of knowledge, and the psychosocial support perceived by the recipient as relevant to work, career, or professional development.

Mentoring entails informal communication, usually face-to-face and during a sustained period of time, between a person who is perceived to have greater relevant knowledge, wisdom, or experience (the mentor) and a person who is perceived to have less (the protégé).

Who is a Mentor?

A mentor is a more experienced professional in your field who offers you career guidance, advice and

"Let us do our best whilst we live for another tomorrow is coming when whilst we are long gone, another group of people shall come to either suffer from our worst or enjoy and build upon our best. Let us run whole heatedly today with all alacrity for another generation shall come for the baton from our hands to either blame us or congratulate us on how we lived the dream and journeyed in life through the good and the bad times; another generation shall come to ponder over our footprints as a good or a bad lesson for them! Let us run with all necessary zeal such that when we hand over the baton, our next generation will have no reason but to soldier on with courage, enthusiasm and absolute commitment to get to the finishing line with a great accomplishment and a noble story worth pondering over and over!"

Ernest Agyemang Yeboah

assistance from a real-world point-of-view. A mentor could also be used to refer to someone who is experienced with life generally and can walk you through your own journey even if that path is not the same as theirs.

Why Should I Bother?

Mentorship offers a host of amazing benefits. A good mentor is wise and willing to share his or her knowledge and experiences in order to help you succeed.

"Having a more experienced and successful counselor guiding someone in a chosen profession is wise decision and good career move."

Jose A. Aviles

It is somewhat similar to having a wonderful trusted ally to go to whenever you are feeling unsure or in need of support. They can be extremely helpful to not only set goals but achieve them, make smart business decisions, overcome workspace challenges. Mentors can even help you learn new skills or simply offer an outside perspective when you are having challenges in the workplace. The benefits can really be endless.

Types of Mentoring

There are two broad types of mentoring relationships: formal and informal. Formal mentoring relationships are set up by an administrative unit or office in a company or organization, which solicits and recruits qualified individuals who are willing to mentor, provides training to the mentors, and then helps to match the mentors up with a person in need of mentoring. While formal mentoring systems contain numerous structural and guidance elements, they still typically allow the mentor and mentee to have an active role in choosing who they want to work with.

Formal mentoring programs which simply assign mentors to mentees without giving these individuals a say have not performed well. Even though a mentor and a mentee may seem perfectly matched "on paper", in practice, they may have different working or learning styles. As such, giving the mentor and the mentee the opportunity to help select who they want to work with is a widely used approach.

Informal mentoring occurs without the use of structured recruitment, mentor training and matching services. Informal mentoring arrangements can develop naturally from business networking situations in which a more experienced individual meets a new employee, and the two strike up a rapport.

"One of the greatest values of mentors are the ability to see ahead what others cannot see and to help them navigate a course to their destination." — John C.

In addition to these broad types, there are also peer, situational and supervisory mentoring relationships. These tend to fall under the categories of formal and informal mentoring relationships. Informal relationships develop on their own between partners. Formal mentoring, on the other hand, refers to a structured process supported by the organization and addressed to target populations.

For example, youth mentoring programs assist at-risk children or youth who lack role models and sponsors. In business, formal mentoring is part of talent management strategies which are used to groom key employees, newly hired graduates, high potential-employees and future leaders. The matching of mentor and mentee is often done by a mentoring coordinator, often with the help of a

> *"The delicate balance of mentoring someone is not creating them in your own image, but giving them the opportunity to create themselves." -Steven Spielberg*

computerized database registry. The use of the database helps to match up mentees with mentors who have the type of experience and qualifications they are seeking.

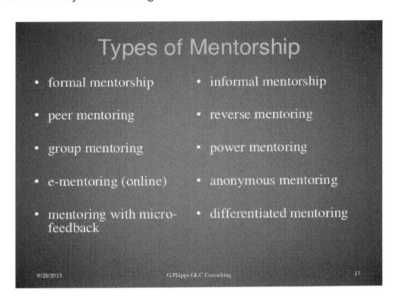

There are formal mentoring programs that are values-oriented, while social mentoring and other types focus specifically on career development. Some mentorship programs provide both social and vocational support. In well-designed formal mentoring programs, there are program goals, schedules, training (for both mentors and protégés), and evaluation.

There are many kinds of mentoring relationships from school or community-based relationships to e-mentoring relationships. These mentoring relationships vary and can be influenced by the type of mentoring relationship that is in effect. That is whether it has come about as a formal or informal relationship. Also, there are several models have been used to describe and examine the sub-relationships that can emerge. For example, Buell describes how mentoring relationships can develop under a cloning model, nurturing model, friendship model and apprenticeship model. The cloning model is about the mentor trying to "produce a duplicate copy of him or herself." The nurturing model takes more of a "parent figure, creating a safe, open environment in which mentee can both learn and try things for him-or herself." The friendship model are more peers "rather than being involved in a hierarchical relationship." Lastly, the apprenticeship is about less "personal or social aspects... and the professional relationship is the sole focus".

"You cannot transit wisdom and insight to another person. The seed is already there. A good teacher touches the seed, allowing it to wake up, to sprout, and to grow."

Thich Nhat Hanh

In the sub-groups of formal and informal mentoring relationships: peer mentoring relationships are relationships where individuals are at the same skill training, similar positions and stages of career. However, one person may be more knowledgeable in a certain aspect or another, but they can help each other to progress in their work. A lot of time, peer relationships provide a lot of support, empathy and advice because the situations are quite similar.

Other Types of Mentoring

Situational mentoring

Short-term relationships in which a person mentors for a specific purpose. This could be a company bringing an expert in regarding social media, or internet safety. This expert can mentor employees to make them more knowledgeable about a specific topic or skill.

> *"YOUR MOST IMPORTANT TASK AS A LEADER IS TO TEACH PEOPLE HOW TO THINK AND ASK THE RIGHT QUESTIONS SO THAT THE WORLD DOESN'T GO TO HELL IF YOU TAKE A DAY OFF"-JEFFREY PFEFFER*

Supervisory Mentoring

This kind of mentoring has 'go to' people who are supervisors. These are people who have answers to many questions and can advise to take the best plan of action. This can be a conflict-of-interest relationship because many supervisors do not feel comfortable also being a mentor.

Mentoring Circles

Participants from all levels of the organization propose and own a topic. They then meet in groups to discuss the topic, which motivates them to grow and become more knowledgeable. Flash mentoring is ideal for job shadowing, reverse mentoring, and more.

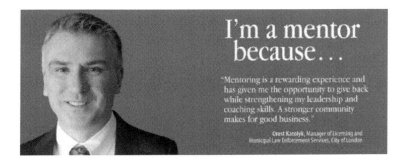

Flash mentoring

Creates a low-pressure environment for mentoring that focuses on single meetings rather than a traditional, long-term mentoring relationship.

Career development

Setting up a career development mentoring program for employees enables an organization to help junior employees to learn the skills and behaviors from senior employees that the junior employees need to advance to higher-responsibility positions. This type of mentoring program can help to align organizational goals with employees' personal career goals (of progressing within the organization). It gives employees the ability to advance professionally and learn more about their work. This collaboration also gives employees a feeling of engagement with the organization, which can lead to better retention rates and increased employee satisfaction.

High potential mentoring

The most talented employees in organizations tend to be difficult to retain, as they are usually seeking greater challenges and responsibilities, and they are likely to leave for a different organization if they do not feel that they are being given the opportunity to develop.

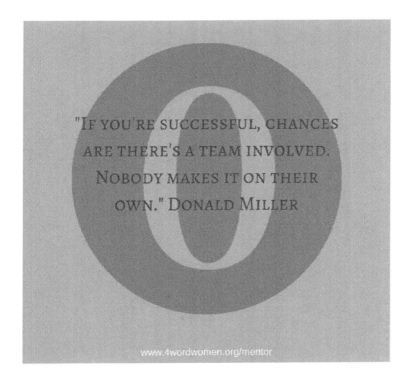

"IF YOU'RE SUCCESSFUL, CHANCES ARE THERE'S A TEAM INVOLVED. NOBODY MAKES IT ON THEIR OWN." DONALD MILLER

www.4wordwomen.org/mentor

Top talent, whether in an innovation or management role, have incredible potential to make great things happen for an organization. Creating a mentoring program for high-potential employees that gives them one-on-one guidance from senior leaders can help to build the engagement of these talented employees, give them the opportunity to develop, and increase their retention in the organization.

———

"A mentor is someone who sees more talent and ability within you, than you see in yourself, and helps bring it out of you." -Bob Proctor

———

Diversity mentoring

One of the top ways to innovate is by bringing in new ideas from senior employees and leaders from underrepresented groups (e.g., women, ethnic minorities, etc.). Who is an underrepresented group depends on the industry sector and country. In many Western countries, women and ethnic minorities are significantly underrepresented in executive positions and boards of directors. In some traditionally gender segregated occupations, such as education and nursing, however, women may be the dominant gender in the workforce.

Mentors from underrepresented groups can empower employees from underrepresented groups to increase their confidence to take on higher-responsibility tasks and prepare for leadership roles. By developing employees from diverse groups, this can give the organization access to new ideas, new ways of looking at problems, and new perspectives. This also brings cultural awareness and intercultural dialogue into the workplace.

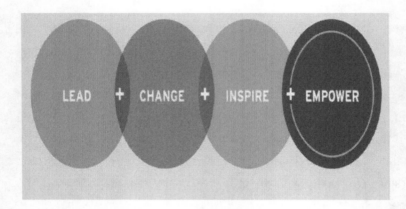

Reverse mentoring

While mentoring typically involves a more experienced, typically older employee or leader providing guidance to a younger employee, the opposite approach can also be used. In the 2000s, with the rise of digital innovations, Internet applications and social media, in some cases, new, young employees are more familiar with these technologies than senior employees in the organizations.

The younger generations can help the older generations to expand and grow towards current trends. Everyone has something to bring to the table, this creates a "two-way street" within companies where younger employees can see the larger picture, and senior employees can learn from young employees.

Knowledge transfer mentoring

Employees must have a certain set of skills in order to accomplish the tasks at hand. Mentoring is a great approach to help employees get organized and give them access to an expert that can give feedback, and help answer questions that they may not know where to find answers to.

Mentorship provides critical benefits to individuals as well as organizations. Although mentorship can be important for an individual's career advancement, in the United States it historically has been most apparent in relation to the advancement of women and minorities in the workplace. Until recent decades, American men in dominant ethnic groups gained most of the benefits of mentorship without consciously identifying it as an advancement strategy. American women and minorities, in contrast, more pointedly identified and pursued mentorship in the second half of the twentieth century as they sought to achieve the professional success they had long been denied.

Techniques in Mentoring

The focus of mentoring is to develop the whole person

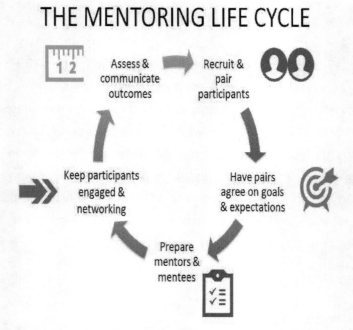

and so the techniques are broad and require wisdom in order to be used appropriately. The most commonly used mentoring techniques in business include this five listed below:

1.   *Accompanying:* making a commitment in a caring way, which involves taking part in the learning process side-by-side with the learner.

2.   *Sowing:* mentors are often confronted with the difficulty of preparing the learner before he or she is ready to change. Sowing is necessary when you know that what you say may not be understood or even acceptable to learners at first but will make sense and have value to the mentee when the situation requires it.

3.   *Catalyzing:* when change reaches a critical level of pressure, learning can escalate. Here the mentor chooses to plunge the learner right into change, provoking a different way of thinking, a change in identity or a re-ordering of values.

Five Phase Mentoring Relationship Model©

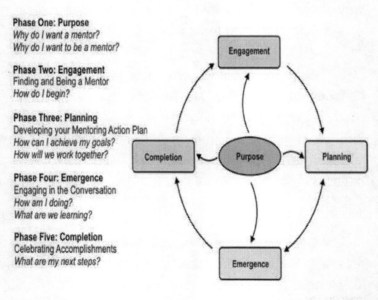

Phase One: Purpose
Why do I want a mentor?
Why do I want to be a mentor?

Phase Two: Engagement
Finding and Being a Mentor
How do I begin?

Phase Three: Planning
Developing your Mentoring Action Plan
How can I achieve my goals?
How will we work together?

Phase Four: Emergence
Engaging in the Conversation
How am I doing?
What are we learning?

Phase Five: Completion
Celebrating Accomplishments
What are my next steps?

Cooper & Wheeler, 2007

4.   *Showing:* this is making something understandable or using your own example to demonstrate a skill or activity. You show what you are talking about, you show by your own behavior.

5.   *Harvesting:* here the mentor focuses on "picking the ripe fruit": it is usually used to create awareness of what was learned by experience and to draw conclusions. The key questions here are: "What have you learned?", "How useful is it?".

Different techniques may be used by mentors according to the situation and the mindset of the mentee, and the techniques used in modern organizations can be found in

...IN 5 KEY STEPS

* Use this 5-step process to deploy a successful mentoring program with true business impact:

Here we go...

ancient education systems, from the Socratic technique of harvesting to the accompaniment method of learning used in the apprenticeship of itinerant cathedral builders during the Middle Ages. Leadership authors Jim Kouzes and Barry Z. Posner advise mentors to look for "teachable moments" in order to "expand or realize the potentialities of the people in the organizations they lead" and underline that personal credibility is as essential to quality mentoring as skill.

Multiple mentors

A new and upcoming trend is having multiple mentors. This can be helpful because we can all learn from each other. Having more than one mentor will widen the knowledge of the person being mentored. There are different mentors who may have different strengths.

Profession or trade mentor

This is someone who is currently in the trade/profession you are entering. They know the trends, important changes and new practices that you should know to stay at the top of your career. A mentor like this would be someone you can discuss ideas regarding the field, and also be introduced to key and important people that you should know.

Industry mentor

92% of women said they felt mentorship or sponsorship was "critical" to their career advancement.

56% of women said a mentor-figure had indeed championed their cause.

43% of women said they sought mentorship for support and guidance on career advancement.

24% of women cited networking as a primary reason for working with a mentor.

*Survey completed by SCN in 2018

This is someone who doesn't just focus on the profession. This mentor will be able to give insight on the industry as a whole. Whether it be research, development or key changes in the industry, you need to know.

Organization mentor

Politics in the organizations are constantly changing. It is important to be knowledgeable about the values, strategies and products that are within your company, but also when these things are changing. An organization mentor can clarify missions, strategies and give clarity when needed.

Work process mentor

This mentor can speed quickly over the bumps and cut through the unnecessary work. This mentor can explain the 'ins and outs' of projects, day to day tasks, and eliminate unnecessary things that may be currently going on in your work day. This mentor can help to get things done quickly and efficiently.

Technology mentor

This is an up-and-coming, incredibly important position. Technology has been rapidly improving and becoming more a part of day-to-day transactions within companies. In order to perform your best, you must know how to get things done on the newest technology. A technology mentor will help with technical breakdowns, advise on systems that may work better than what you're currently using, and coach you through new technology and how to best use it and implement it into your daily life.

These mentors are only examples. There can be many more different types of mentors. Look around your workplace, your life, and see who is an expert that you can learn something from.

Why Seek Out a Mentor?

I attribute part of my professional growth to the guidance of a patient mentor. He challenged me to think differently and to open my eyes and mind to different perspectives. While each of us develops at our own pace, it is reasonable to believe that this type of influence is positive for all of us.

A mentor is a personal advocate for you, not so much in the public setting, but rather in your life. Many organizations recognize the power of effective mentoring and have established programs to help younger professionals identify and gain support from more experienced professional in this format.

What's in it for Them?

You are probably reading all of this thinking, "I get why I should want a mentor. But what's in it for them?" The answer is different for everyone.

Some mentors simply believe in the person they are helping and want to see him or her succeed, and that alone is worth the time and energy. Others look at mentorship as a way of leaving a legacy- giving back to life. As a mentor, they can pass their wisdom down to the next generation rather than dying with it and let someone re-invent the wheel.

Some people also do it because it has the power to make a huge difference in the industry or company where they work and even the world at large.

When Should I Get a Mentor?

Mentors are helpful regardless of where you are in your career. Whether you're fresh out of college or a few years

"One of the greatest values of mentors is the ability to see ahead what others cannot see and to help them navigate a course to their destination"

-JOHN C. MAXWELL

from retirement, there are always others who have "been there, done that" from whom you can learn. So, no matter who you are, I always say, "NOW is a great time to start."

If or when you're more experienced, you may want to BE a mentor. Please do so!! It's an incredibly fulfilling experience and I believe that mentors learn just as much as those they assist. But I encourage everyone to also find a mentor of your own. As humans, we're always learning and evolving, and even the most experienced professional doesn't know everything.

More than likely, the mentorship relationships of experienced professionals will not look the same as those who are entry-level or mid-career. You may have a mentor who is closer in age and experience—or even someone who is your junior! As long as the person has qualities and knowledge you can learn from, it's perfectly acceptable.

CHAPTER TWO
ATTRACTING GREAT MENTORS

"Search for role models you can look up to and people who take an interest in your career. But here's an important warning: you don't have to have mentors who look like you. Had I been waiting for a black, female Soviet specialist mentor, I would still be waiting. Most of my mentors have been old white men, because they were the ones who dominated my field." Condoleeza Rice

There are many ways to attract great mentors who will be willing to expedite your time on the learning curve. However, it is important to note that mentoring relationships need to be rewarding for both parties. What this means is that the mentee shouldn't be the sole beneficiary of the relationship. The mentor should get some sort of value for the time and effort he is putting into the mentoring relationship.

"

Make no mistake; your greatest teacher will not be what you expect. Your mentor will embody love, light, grace, and compassion. However, your greatest teacher comes imbued with rage, darkness, fear, and judgment.

It is when you have overcome the trials of your greatest teacher, with the tools of your mentor, you will finally recognize the truth.

You are both them, and they are both you.

This is the hero's journey.

stace morris

Ways Mentors Help You Succeed

Mentorship is not limited to just business or general life principles; it applies to career too. Most successful career people will tell you that mentors made a big difference in their careers.

Their mentorship may not always translate into breaking through the glass ceiling, but mentors can help your work performance, help you achieve success in a company and also help you be more fulfilled in your work.

"We're here for a reason. I believe a bit of the reason is to throw little torches out to lead people through the dark."

-Whoopi Goldberg

Here are 11 ways a mentor can help you during four general stages of your career:

Stage 1: Newbie

Your mentors can help you acclimatize to a new job or work environment in the following ways, because they have run through the ranks.

- Finding Your Way and Learning the Rules: Bonnie Marcus, author of *The Politics of Promotion*, says, "The mentor can offer advice on how to best navigate in the new work environment and give information about the people and politics." A mentor within your company can help you understand corporate expectations—both spoken and unspoken rules. They can point out mistakes if they see you in action. Your mentor can help you feel comfortable operating within a new environment.

- Identify your skill set and anything missing that you need to work on. In my second job out of business school, a mentor suggested I attend trainings in time management and organization, which helped me to be more effective in my job.

> The learning and knowledge
> that we have is, at the most,
> but little compared with that
> of which we are ignorant.
>
> -Plato

- Model That Works: Ask your mentors to share their stories of what has worked in their careers and what hasn't. Learn from your mentors' experience. Beth B. Kennedy, a leadership coach who has taught many leaders how to begin a successful mentoring relationship, shares the success of a client whose mentor taught her "excellent delegation and time management strategies" that led to the client's success and promotion.

Stage 2: Strategy

Your mentors can help you draft out a plan for building your career and how to get there along the following lines:

- Create a Vision: A mentor can help you think through where you want to go with your career in the long run and how you can get there. This type of mentor can be someone in your workplace or in your field, or more of a general business coach, perhaps even someone you hire.

- Look for Resonance: A mentor or coach can help you assess how well your current environment fits your values, skills and interests. You will be happier with a job and environment that resonates with your ability and capability.

- Help You Define Success: Long term success is not only about what a company or environment defines as success, says Amy Beilharz, former corporate executive turned serial entrepreneur and business coach. She points out group goals, relationships and contribution to a larger cause as important elements to feeling fulfilled in your career.

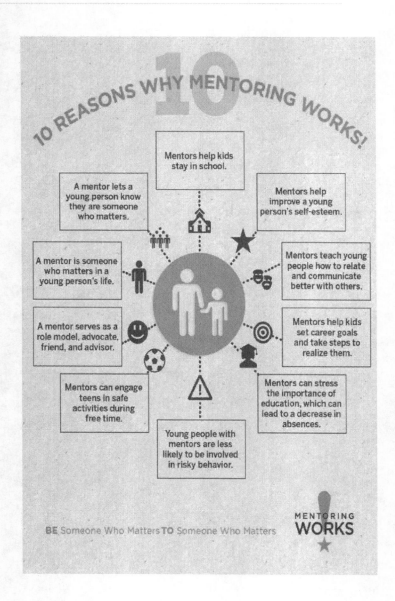

Stage 3: Mobile

As you go through your career and life in general, you will come across crossroads and points where you urgently need to make a decision. At these points, your mentors provide support in these forms:

- Solve Problems: You can turn to your mentors for feedback on any projects you are undertaking or handling. They could also offer possible solutions to problems, as well as general strategies that have worked for them in similar situations.

- Evaluate Job Offers: You may be offered a job within your own department, another part of the company or even a different company. Sometimes it's hard to see all the ramifications of taking a particular job—both for short-term fit and also for its long-term strategic value, especially when the offer comes with nice perks.

A mentor can help you see all angles and evaluate the fit. You may stand a chance of earning better with a new offer but not advance in your career goals and a mentor can help you see that loop.

Stage 4: Successful

At the end of the day, everyone wants to achieve their goals, advance and become successful. However, success is not just magic wand that falls in your hands. You have to walk the journey to success with its principles as compass. Here are some ways mentors help you achieve success:

- Help You Network: Marcus says mentors can introduce mentees "to potential allies and champions."
- Get You Noticed: Beth B. Kennedy, a leadership coach who has taught many leaders how to achieve success through mentoring relationship recounts a story, "A current client of mine learned strategies from her mentor that led to her promotion.

Her mentor taught her ways to raise her visibility in an authentic way. Another practical example here is Bishop Oyedepo and Sam Adeyemi in ministry. As Sam would always say, "where I was before meeting my mentor is little compared to where I am now keeping relationship with my Mentor Bishop David Oyedepo!"

- Mentors Can Serve as Sponsors: Marcus points out

> *"In a battery, I strive to maximize electrical potenti*
> *When mentoring, I strive to maximize human*
> *potential"*
>
> *-Donald Sadoway*

that at the upper echelons, it's not just about mentoring. Mentors can help mentees get promoted and move forward in their career by introducing and suggesting them for promotion to the right people or organizations that have a need for their skill set. It is easier for people to trust and want to work with you when someone more experienced is spreading the word about you.

- External Opportunities: Mentors in your field can help you look beyond your company for opportunities. They may help you decide what you are looking for, introduce you to contacts of theirs, or even help you get into their own organizations.

Finding A Mentor

Cultivate mentors within your company and outside of it. Kennedy offers the possibility of someone "from a different department to add a more systemic and strategic perspective." Your boss can also be a good mentor, depending on the person.

Mentorship is not rocket science and she goes further to say, "The best mentoring relationships take place when they're not forced mentoring programs. A proactive way to get a mentor is to begin the process in a more unofficial way."

My mentors in life are much older than me and have been through life. They can actually give me some sound advice on what I'm going through.
~Nicole Trunfio

topfamousquotes.com

How?

- Identify someone who has been successful in your organization or field in a way that resonates with you or that has certain skills and relationships you'd like to emulate.

- Get to know them. Kennedy suggests you ask for a brief meeting over coffee or visiting their occasions as the case may be in Nigeria, nothing fancy. You could tell them the reason for the meeting is just to ask a few questions or their opinion on some projects.

- Kennedy says, "Asses the synergy." What does your gut tell you about the mentor? "Does the possible mentor have the time and energy to mentor?"

- After a few casual meetings, Kennedy says you can then ask the person if they would be your mentor.

"Share your expectations. Some of the best mentoring relationships my clients have shared with me are the relationships that meet once a month and the mentee brings questions and an agenda. The mentee needs to be proactive and discuss their needs." It's also a good idea to share articles on mentoring and "other best practices with your mentor."

- At some point you want to evaluate the effectiveness. Kennedy suggests an assessment six months or a year down the road. If it's not working, you can thank your mentor and move on to someone new.

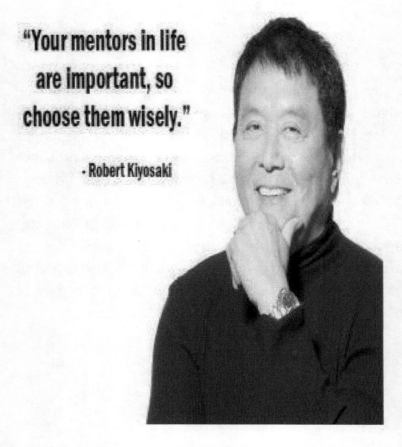

"Your mentors in life are important, so choose them wisely."

- Robert Kiyosaki

Most importantly, don't just sit waiting for someone to offer to mentor you. Start to think now about specific ways you want a mentor to help you and list people who might be of help. It would look foolish to meet a potential mentor and cannot state practical areas and how you need mentoring.

You can have more than one mentor at a time, too. If you still have no idea how it would all work, you could ask other people about their mentoring experiences, as well. And if your company has a mentoring program, find out how one gets chosen to participate. Really, no one goes it alone in the corporate world. The support of your mentors can be one of the most important determinants in your success.

CHAPTER THREE

CHOOSING A MENTOR

"What I think the mentor gets is the great satisfaction of helping somebody along, helping somebody take advantage of an opportunity that maybe he or she did not have." — Clint Eastwood

This is a big question and I recommend you take some time to think it over carefully. The choice of person makes a significant difference in the success of the relationship and, ultimately, in your success. Look for someone you respect professionally and someone who has a career you'd like to emulate. That doesn't mean you want to follow in their footsteps *exactly*; you're just looking for a person who has had success in your field (or even a similar one) and someone who embodies the professional characteristics you're working to achieve.

Of course, you also need to find someone who is willing to be a mentor, is eager to share knowledge, will be open and honest with you, will have time to dedicate to you (though how much is flexible) and is trustworthy. You'll be potentially sharing a lot of sensitive information, so this last point is essential.

I recommend that you look for someone you like on a personal level, not just a professional one. You should look forward to spending time with your mentor. The conversations should be pleasant, engaging and inspiring.

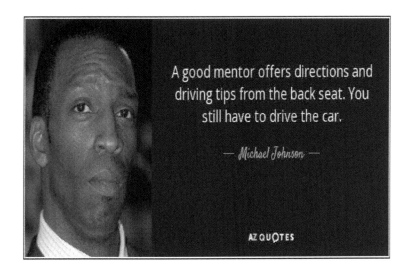

A good mentor offers directions and driving tips from the back seat. You still have to drive the car.

— Michael Johnson —

AZ QUOTES

Who Should Be My Mentor?

The word mentor is defined as both a noun ("a trusted counselor or guide") and a verb ("to serve as a mentor for"). The idea of "mentorship" for most of us in veterinary medicine defines a process that combines both applications of the word.

At various points in our lives, we all identify and seek to learn from, and often emulate, our mentors. They become models for the development of proper problem solving and decision-making techniques, the demonstration of technical skills, developing interpersonal abilities, and providing personal guidance. Mentors and the idea of mentorship has taken on increased awareness in veterinary medicine today, particularly among new veterinary graduates and new practice owners who are dropped suddenly into new and unfamiliar roles and face the challenge of high expectations, information overload, and little time to learn to become master of all tasks.

Veterinary schools, ironically, face the same challenges in attempting to educate veterinary students. While veterinary students graduate with sound knowledge and adequate or higher entry level technical skills, the schools cannot be expected to send them into their new roles as practitioners with a complete and versed set of skills and coping abilities. Individual graduates also enter the workplace with differing levels of confidence and experience, thus creating great variability in their need for mentoring.

The need for further education and training, therefore, continues for some time following graduation; it is significantly influenced by the willingness of experienced veterinarians to teach and coach, and by the confidence and willingness of the new graduate to listen and take direction.

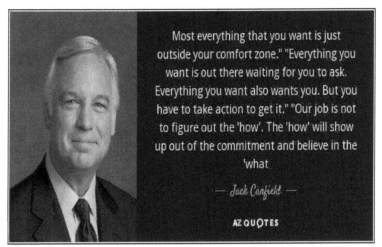

Most everything that you want is just outside your comfort zone." "Everything you want is out there waiting for you to ask. Everything you want also wants you. But you have to take action to get it." "Our job is not to figure out the 'how'. The 'how' will show up out of the commitment and believe in the 'what.

— *Jack Canfield* —

AZ QUOTES

The stumbling block in many mentoring relationships is in defining exactly what mentorship means to the individuals involved. The interpretation of mentorship is largely subjective, so the process and contents of this activity need to be defined at its inception for it to be effective for both parties. If there is no open communication between mentors and pupils, expectations could be set unrealistically on both sides of the relationship, so that frustrations will mount, performance will be affected, and, inevitably, many of the relationships will dissolve unnecessarily.

New or recent graduates or associates with one or more areas that they feel require further development or improved problem-solving abilities should be encouraged to identify these areas openly; they should not perceive them as weaknesses that they should hide and somehow try to correct or improve on their own, but as areas that once developed and refined will help the practice to achieve its goals.

It is conceivable that some new graduates, particularly those lacking confidence, may be seeking some continuance of the student environment, where they received reinforcement and observation on most things they did in the hospital. Others who are extremely independent from the beginning simply need to know that the voice of assistance is but a phone call or yell for help away.

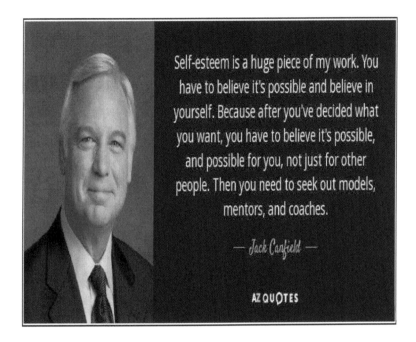

Self-esteem is a huge piece of my work. You have to believe it's possible and believe in yourself. Because after you've decided what you want, you have to believe it's possible, and possible for you, not just for other people. Then you need to seek out models, mentors, and coaches.

— Jack Canfield —

AZ QUOTES

Practice owners or more seasoned veterinary mentors and coaches should define how they propose to bring about the transition of a new veterinarian into the practice, what they expect, in terms of feedback, with respect to difficulties the new veterinarian is experiencing, what the ascending levels of responsibility and challenge for new veterinarians will be, and who individual or multiple mentors are and when they will be accessible for questions, conversation, and hands-on guidance, if necessary. Employers should also set some kind of reasonable timeline or end date with respect to performance goals for these new employees. While mentorship is an ongoing process, it should taper off in its intensity and, therefore, is not an endless process.

Focus groups that I conduct annually among new graduates always identify one of their largest frustrations as being the scenario where a new graduate is thrust into a practice on day 1 with either an absent owner or an experienced veterinarian being unavailable to them, or, even more frustratingly, being on site but simply having no time.

The concept of being part of a team working towards a collective goal is quickly lost in these settings, which is a key factor leading towards the unnecessarily high turnover rates that the veterinary profession has among new graduates. While formal continuing education gatherings can always play a valuable role for veterinarians of any experience level, the issue with newer graduates is often simply in having someone available to reinforce their decisions and thus help them to build confidence and establish a sound frame of reference for the future.

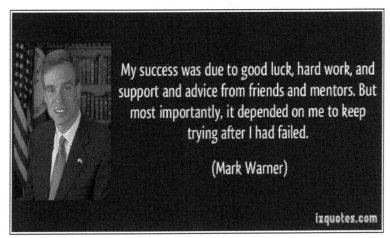

My success was due to good luck, hard work, and support and advice from friends and mentors. But most importantly, it depended on me to keep trying after I had failed.

(Mark Warner)

izquotes.com

The goal of any mentorship activities should be to create an environment that allows new associates to progress as rapidly as possible along the learning curve and mature their practice skills. That environment can be formalized in discussions leading to defining the terms of employment or later in writing by creating an employment contract with new associates.

New associates are generally pleased to have the terms of their mentorship defined, as those requiring more intensive mentorship feel that easing into full responsibilities and decision making provides a temporary security net for them and sets a more comfortable level of what is expected during the initial phase of their employment. Wording to define mentorship in an employment contract can be captured by defining progressive independent scheduling and responsibilities, defining time and/or activities spent working directly with other veterinarians, establishing regular times for meetings during the workweek, scheduling a performance review or reviews at specific periods over the duration of the contract, when the mentorship activities can be reviewed and tapered off in their intensity as the new associate progresses.

The issue is much the same for new practice owners, who now have the multiple issues of running a business to deal with, in addition to the actual practice. If a new owner or owners are inside the practice already, hopefully much of that mentorship has happened by observation and a sharing of the business activities.

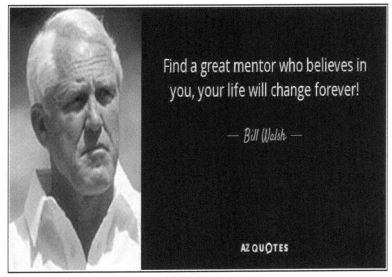

Find a great mentor who believes in you, your life will change forever!

— Bill Walsh —

AZ QUOTES

For purchasers coming from outside the practice, transition with an outgoing vendor is important both for maintaining the culture of the business and for helping to guide the new owner(s) with respect to the management and leadership of the practice.

How Does the Mentorship Relationship Work?

Establish specifics around your relationship in whatever way works best for both you and your mentor. It can be a formal arrangement, an informal one or something in the middle. No matter what, it has to work for both of you. To get started, I recommend that you, as the mentee, come up with your "ideal" relationship. Share the information with your mentor and make sure you leave it open for discussion. Find out how much time they are willing to invest and build a schedule based on that.

For example, my first mentorship relationship was rather informal. My mentor and I would meet via phone about once a month (usually for an hour) and in between these conversations, we would communicate via email. I would send work to him when I needed a quick critique. He would send me links of articles to read when he stumbled upon something I might learn from.

> *"Every great achiever
> is inspired
> by a great mentor."*
>
> — Lailah Gifty Akita

When I was facing a challenge, I would check in with him for a little guidance and reassurance that I was doing the right thing. A few times a year, he would send me a book.

It was an easy relationship for both of us to keep up with, but I got tremendous benefit from it.

The key to success is simply defining the relationship from the beginning. Make it an open dialogue. Ask for what you want and need from your mentor, be willing to compromise, and listen closely to make sure there is agreement. Be sure to clarify your expectations (specifically around things like confidentiality). You don't want there to be any confusion.

Lastly, let your mentor know that you see this as an ongoing process. If, at any time, the relationship isn't working for either one of you, the details can and should be reviewed and revised. This doesn't have to be stressful like a contract negotiation. Remember, it's supposed to be a fun, growth experience!

Better than a
thousand days of
diligent study is
one day with a
great teacher.
-*Japanese Proverb*

CHAPTER FOUR

GIVING BACK TO YOUR MENTOR

"A lot of people put pressure on themselves and think it will be way too hard for them to live out their dreams. Mentors are there to say, 'Look, it's not that tough. It's not as hard as you think. Here are some guidelines and things I have gone through to get to where I am in my career.'" — *Joe Jonas*

It is not uncommon for mentees to suppose that they don't have anything to provide to their mentor. And that is not true. You might have the financial capability to get little gifts for them but then you also might not.

Below are a few ways you can give value back to your mentor:

- **Gratitude**

At the simplest stage, mentors need to know that they are making a distinction in your life. Or what is the point of a mentor expending his resources- time, knowledge and maybe research to give you tailored advice- and you are not the better for it?

So, let your mentor know how they've made a distinction in your life. And don't just say the cliches "you have helped me become better". Be particular. Tell them how a technique or advice they gave helped you achieve something. Now, that is progress and impact for them!

After each meeting with you, your mentors ought to take

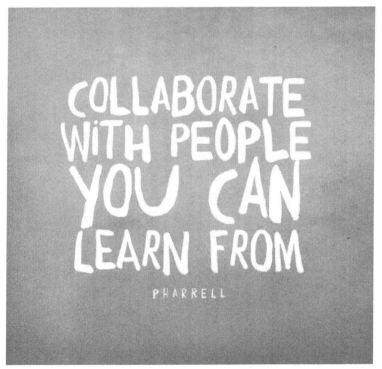

away a feeling of accomplishment. That is the reason why they lend an helping hand.

- ### Public Mentions

Another means you can also give value to your mentors is through public mentioning. As you and your organization become extra profitable or more profitable than you were, talk about them in public, on social media and even give them referrals.

If you read books, you may discover that some authors acknowledge their mentors and influencers by identifying and making reference to them. They'll do that not simply within the "acknowledgements," however within the core of the book itself.

- ### Being Successful

Being successful, becoming terribly profitable, in the area you are being mentored is the ultimate way to say "thanks" to a mentor. Mentors want to know that they made a distinction in your life and that their contribution helped you hit your objectives.

Mentors wish to make a distinction on this planet. If you go from beginning a new enterprise to being a profitable entrepreneur because of your mentors, they're going to really feel very fulfilled. They'll be glad they mentored you. So, go the extra mile to produce results with their lessons.

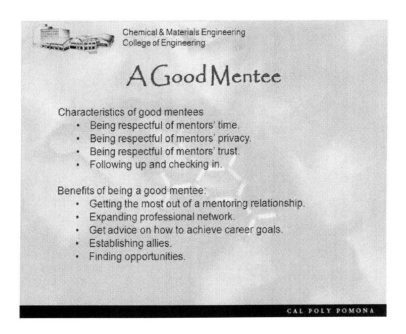

- **Add Value**

Don't view your mentorship relationships as you just taking from them. View it as a mutual relationship, the place they need to make a distinction and you as their conduit.

Make yourself available for their programs, events or conferences. If you can help out with the logistics of their event, jump in and help out.

CHAPTER FIVE

STARTUP INCUBATOR OR ACCELERATOR

"Show me a successful individual and I'll show you someone who had real positive influences in his or her life. I don't care what you do for a living—if you do it well I'm sure there was someone cheering you on or showing the way. A mentor." – Denzel Washington

One way to help get your business off the ground, is to leverage the mentorship and investor relationship benefits of a startup incubator or an accelerator. First of all, what is the difference between an incubator and an accelerator?

A Startup Incubator

An incubator is physically locating your business in one central work space with many other startup companies. In many cases, the startups in these incubators can all be venture funded by the same investor group. You can stay in the space as long as you need to, until your business has grown to the scale it needs to relocate to its own space or depending on the terms.

The mentorship is typically provided by proven entrepreneurial investors, and by shared learnings of your startup CEO peers. Examples include Lightbank and

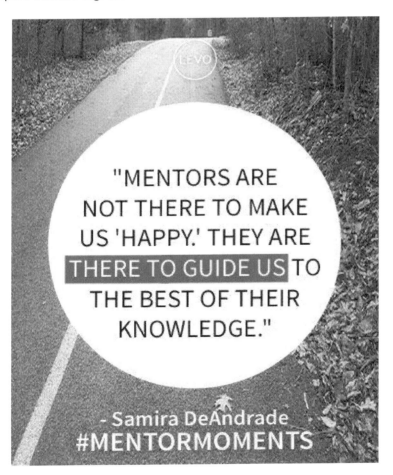

"MENTORS ARE NOT THERE TO MAKE US 'HAPPY.' THEY ARE THERE TO GUIDE US TO THE BEST OF THEIR KNOWLEDGE."

- Samira DeAndrade
#MENTORMOMENTS

Sandbox Industries in Chicago. And SME HOUSE by Stephen Akintayo in Nigeria

Startup incubators are referred to occasionally as "business school," and that's certainly a strong focus on the best options. Leading incubators take entrepreneurs with promising ideas, and teach them how to run a successful startup and help to validate the business ideas coming out of incubators. Typical benefits might include guidance and resources, funding opportunities, and a credibility boost from membership.

Incubators do not traditionally provide capital to startups and are often funded by universities or economic development organizations. They also don't usually take an equity stake in the companies they support but charge a fee to participate in their incubator program. Some incubators however take equity around 12% and below.

Incubators tend to take on startups which are still in formation, may not necessarily require investment capital and tend to be part of the local startup community already. The timeline to commercialization may be longer, or they are so early that some of the basics have not been addressed yet.

> # A mentor empowers a person to see a possible future, and believe it can be obtained.
> — Shawn Hitchcock

A Startup Accelerator?

There's certainly overlap between accelerators and incubators, but the difference is in the stage of startups they accept. Sepulveda views incubators as a tool for the "childhood" of a startup, while accelerators can guide entrepreneurs from "adolescence to adulthood."

Since accelerators' members already have a minimum viable product (MVP) their resources are often focused on operations and strategy, management coaching, and branding.

Accelerators are generally designed to be a short-term option for fledgling startups, with membership terms ranging from 3-6 months. Once again, the stage of your startup is a top factor in your decision to explore this space as they basically jumpstart your business before kicking you out. In fact, some people even believe joining accelerators at the wrong stage is dangerous.

Accelerators invest a specific amount of capital in startups in exchange for a predetermined percentage of equity. Usually, the cash investment into your business from the accelerator itself usually ranges between $10,000-$20,000/ N5,000,000), but your time in the accelerator should largely improve your chances of raising venture capital from a third-party entity affiliated to the accelerator the program ends.

Mentorship could also come from entrepreneurs affiliated with the accelerator (many of which are proven CEOs, or investors looking for their next opportunity or simply helping the local startup community). Examples include Tech Stars and Y Combinator.

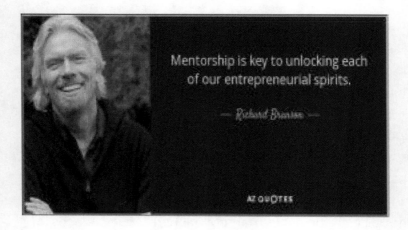

Finding co-founders and key team members can take a while, but accelerators are not meant for that task.

Both incubators and accelerators offer an environment of collaboration and mentorship. This enables the startups to share a space, as well as have access to a multitude of resources and peer feedback.

Are These Programs Right for You?

Deciding on whether or not you should pursue starting up your business via an incubator or accelerator largely comes down to your personal confidence in the feasibility of your business model, your execution skills and your fund-raising skills. If you have a credible story and your business is nicely progressing on your own, you probably don't need to be part of one of these programs. But, if you need help fine tuning your business model or revenue model, or may be a first time CEO wanting to hone your skills from proven peers and entrepreneurs, then this type of mentorship could be perfect for you. When deciding which program is right for their startup, entrepreneurs should look for the right fit. Most startups could benefit from being in an incubator, but fewer are a fit for an accelerator.

The Advantages?

- Shared learnings and mentorship (helping avoid typical startup pitfalls and speeding up your efforts)
- Access to capital, either within an incubator or post an accelerator
- The PR value and exposure you get from these programs (not to be underestimated).

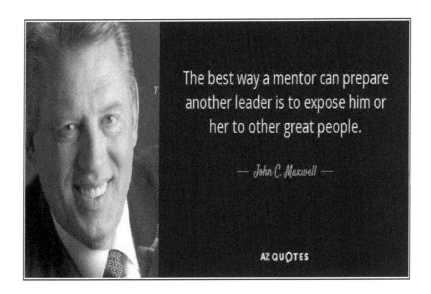

The Disadvantages?

- They can cause distraction, at times, with lots of related meetings and events with mentors and investors (getting in the way of focusing on your own project)

- They can be confusing at times (getting 10 different opinions from 10 different mentors), so you need a good "filter" on any advice.
- Sometimes, sharing space with other companies is not always a plus, especially in long term incubators that may be carrying dead weight of under-performing companies.

On the overall, incubators could be terrific for first time CEOs, in quickly getting them up the learning curve with the help of mentors and investors that have "been there and done that". Plus, your odds of raising capital are vastly improved given the tight screening processes of these groups, that churn out disruptive brands from the sheer number of applicants they receive each year.

Competition is naturally fierce to get one of these coveted spots, so make sure you have a fine-tuned pitch and leverage your network to help pull some strings for you.

And, if you don't get accepted into a startup accelerator or incubator, it is not the end of the world. You could always pay for a co-working space in an incubator, meet other start-up founders like you while learning the little you can.

The Mentor

*People who grew up in difficult circumstances and yet are successful
have one thing in common; at a crucial juncture in their
adolescence, they had a positive relationship with a caring adult
- Bill Clinton, President of the United States*

CHAPTER SIX

BOARD MEMBERS/BUSINESS MENTORS

Mentoring brings us together - across generation, class, and often race - in a manner that forces us to acknowledge our interdependence, to appreciate, in Martin Luther King, Jr.'s words, that 'we are caught in an inescapable network of mutuality, tied to a single garment of destiny.' In this way, mentoring enables us to participate in the essential but unfinished drama of reinventing community, while reaffirming
that there is an important role for each of us in it. Marc Freedman

I had an unfortunate and preventable misunderstanding with a young founder whom had a great idea. I had a mentor/mentee relationship with him. The cause of the misunderstanding, which initially was quite heated, stemmed from an uncommunicated misalignment of expectation. Our relationship and the business evolved from nothing but a raw idea with some early positive feedback from its future user group on *Facebook* into a full-fledged business model and extremely well built and completely scalable MVP. I wouldn't go into details but I realized this scenario has a lot to do with the confusion in the marketplace for young or first-time founders as it relates to the distinctions, similarities and compensation norms for three key roles that are mentor, board advisors, and board directors.

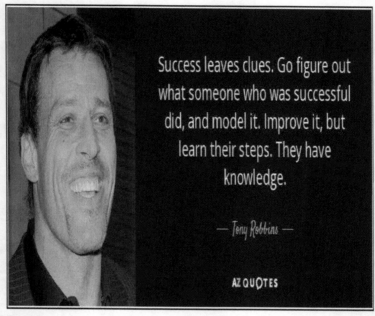

Success leaves clues. Go figure out what someone who was successful did, and model it. Improve it, but learn their steps. They have knowledge.

— Tony Robbins —

AZ QUOTES

The Mentor

They are committed and generous with advice, experience, and assistance or introductions, but is usually informal with no formal compensation or contract or deliverables. Most prolific and valuable mentors don't purposefully use their relationship as bait to hook into a sales strategy or paid engagement with their mentees for consulting services. This doesn't prevent transactional relationships from occurring or evolving from the initial mentor/mentee dynamic, it merely means that the intention of the initial relationship is not transactional or with an agenda more powerful than the one to give, help, and support the innovator and their business to get on some level track.

To the entrepreneur a wide variety of mentors is a good asset to acquire and often because, although you may get several conflicting opinions on the same topics or question (i.e. mentor whiplash), it deepens your network, allows for a great experience in critical thinking, evaluation, and decision making, and builds confidence in listening but also trusting your gut and living with the outcomes.

Essentially, the value of being a mentor is to truly give back to your fellow entrepreneurs in a spirit of pure generosity and because you have walked in shoes they have not and can lend them insights into the road ahead, the lifestyle, the potholes to avoid, and be a model of resilience they can latch onto or reach out to when times are tough and they feel alone.

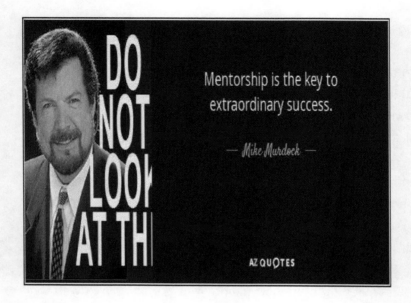

This sort of relationship is completely organic and unpredictable. Some mentor/mentee relationships begin and end over a 20-minute session during a startup week and others can go off and on informally and develop into meaningful professional and personal peer-to-peer relationships.

In some cases, the mentor is part of a pool of mentors in some accelerators that carve up a piece of their equity as part of their contract and award a portion of it to the mentors in the form of bulk portfolio or cohort warrants.

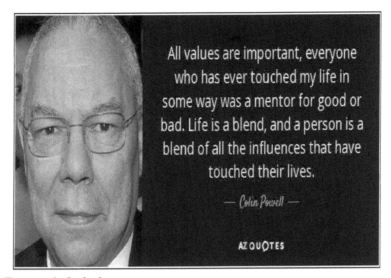

All values are important, everyone who has ever touched my life in some way was a mentor for good or bad. Life is a blend, and a person is a blend of all the influences that have touched their lives.

— Colin Powell —

AZ QUOTES

The Board Advisor

With the board advisor, the relationship is more formal but not legally authorized to bind the corporation. As companies move through the lean canvas or business model design from idea to MVP they will typically begin to formalize several things including their entity formation, capital access strategy and issue founders stock and set up the initial bylaws to prepare for full scale operations and initial sales or capital raising activity.

It is at this point that certain domain experts (many of whom may have mentored the founder or company earlier or have been introduced by a mentor to the company because of a key need that surfaced), become valuable and needed to advance towards an established early milestone.

At the same time it is also common that formalizing with legal authority outside directors on the company's board is pre-mature for one or both parties. This is where the advisory role is a key asset to attract and formalize to a specific degree with regards to what type of help, access, time commitment, and introductions are requested and what type of compensation (typically small portions of equity depending on the stage of the business) is offered in exchange.

For a highly used and fair and quick template agreement I suggest something like the *FAST agreement template by Founders Institute as a great starting point for companies and potential advisors to work from and use to save time, align expectations, and avoid confusion.

To A Special Teacher

When I started in school,
This day seemed so far away.

Now it's here and I can't believe
That time has passed so quickly...

But through your encouragement and guidance,
I feel I'm ready for tomorrow's challenges.

Teachers play such an important part
in shaping and guiding...
Especially teachers like you,
Thank you for caring so much.

You should consider the following professionals for your advisory board; a legal professional, an accountant, a marketing expert, a human resources expert and perhaps a financial advisor. You may also want successful entrepreneurs from other industries who understand the basics of business and will view your operation with a fresh eye.

And be clear about what you are trying to do when setting up an advisory board- how else can they be of help if they don't have a clear picture of your business? Let your prospective advisors know what your business goals are and that you don't expect them to take on an active management role or assume any liability for your company or for the advice they offer.

JANUARY IS

MENTORING MONTH

As a small business owner, there's no need to feel alone. Mentors can provide valuable advice and assistance and help small business owners on their way to success.

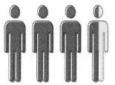

88%
OF BUSINESS OWNERS WITH A MENTOR SAY HAVING ONE IS **INVALUABLE**

SMALL BUSINESSES THAT RECEIVE MENTORING ARE

20%
MORE LIKELY TO EXPERIENCE
GROWTH
THAN THOSE THAT DON'T

70%
of small businesses that receive mentoring stay in business FOR FIVE YEARS OR MORE **WHICH IS 2X MORE** THAN NON-MENTORED BUSINESSES

SMALL BUSINESS CLIENTS WHO RECEIVE *3+ HOURS* OF MENTORING REPORT HIGHER REVENUES AND **INCREASED BUSINESS** GROWTH

54%
of small business owners say they would CONSIDER MENTORING SOMEONE ELSE

98%
of small business owners WOULD RECOMMEND HAVING A MENTOR to other business owners

The UPS Store® is proud to work with SCORE, "Mentors to America's Small Businesses" in supporting small business owners across America. For more information about how The UPS Store and SCORE can support your small business or to find a mentor near you, visit: www.theupsstore.com/score

The UPS Store

WE ♡ LOGISTICS

Results based on a survey of The UPS Store small business customers. To learn more about the survey visit TheUPSStore.com/score

Compensation for advisory board members are more with kind, maybe cash if you can afford it or in some few cases equity silvers, depending on the agreement. Being on your board benefits them in a variety of tangible and intangible ways like exposing them to ideas and perspectives they may have otherwise missed. It will also expand their own networks, which can offer a wide range of advantages.

Back to my story, here is the lessons learned. The founder (who was my mentee) received printed and digital docs of the FAST agreement and we discussed needing to customize it and agree on where in the bucket my expertise fell regarding reasonable equity grant to continue, BUT what I never knew until after the blowup is despite nodding and agreeing to finalize and discuss, the founder never actually even read the 4 pages to have any idea of what the FAST agreement actually was. And that was the genesis of the disagreement. I assumed that the multiple touch points and discussions had us operating from a clear sense of the terms and language and matrices within it and that we were just looking for the time to sit down and nail down the final language and amounts to execute.

Please, DON'T assume or promote someone on your slide deck as such if you are the founder until you have sat down to talk over an agreement, gone through why this evolution of the relationship makes sense, what the scope of work, perceived value and equity grant and any vesting schedule will be.

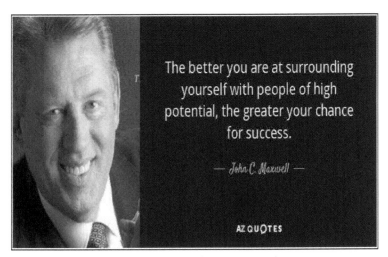

The value of a board advisor can be tremendous as you move your business to a more formal and operational entity. It can round out holes in the founding team from

"You know, you do need mentors, but in the end, you really just need to believe in yourself"
-Diana Ross

both experienced and technical expertise as well as help 'recruit' key resources, players, and potential capital providers to conversations around your opportunity. All of this and more while at the same time keeping your legal governance close to the vest until the time for establishing true CEO compensation and term sheet evaluation or shareholder value metrics and management oversight comes.

Board of Advisors are more flexible and less time consuming than board of directors and can be fluid in its duration where it exists ongoing in parallel to the Board of Directors for specific outside value or as a stair step to a formal board run company.

The Board Director

The relationship of a board director is that of a formal officer of the corporation with binding and fiduciary responsibility to the shareholders of the company and the ability to hire/fire the CEO of the company and approve or deny major capital raises, acquisitions and key hires.

When scouting or trying to choose board members, it is important to select independent person who do not have a vested interest in the company i.e. those that are not exactly affiliated. So, instead of selecting a shareholder or an existing investor, select neutral persons who will do their best to make your business better rather than act based on what they stand to gain.

As your company moves into commercialization the value of an both an advisory board and inside board of directors formalizes many of the necessary management processes by which you will build enterprise value, establish and measure governance and performance for the investors. It also serves as an important way to establish and speed up the relationships and key account activity or capital raising efforts as you select board members who have deep and credible relationships that become available to the company more formally as your move ahead.

MENTORS HAVE A WAY OF SEEING MORE OF OUR FAULTS THAT WE WOULD LIKE.

It's the only way to grow.

GEORGE LUCAS

A formal board of directors (remember you as the CEO and founder, the co-founder/COO are executive directors and will be part of the board when you institute a board of directors) is typically not needed at the early stage in private companies but becomes necessary as you seek bigger funding and become a bigger enterprise. Compensation for board of directors depends on the stage of the company and company legal agreements but it usually is in several forms that typically combine equity with vesting schedules and cash or reimbursements for reasonable related expenses and time.

Ultimately, relationships are made up of millions of points of communication in verbal, written, and subject to the interpretation and filter of each listener. The entrepreneurial journey of taking nothing into something and something into something BIG requires a constant evolution and lots of inputs and people. Hopefully this will allow for a better discussion and clarity between those helping and those needing help, so that frustration and or disappointment can be mitigated more frequently

CHAPTER SEVEN

BUILDING A TEAM OF INFORMAL

MENTORS

"A lot of people put pressure on themselves and think it will be way too hard for them to live out their dreams. Mentors are there to say, 'Look, it's not that tough. It's not as hard as you think. Here are some guidelines and things I have gone through to get to where I am in my career.'" — Joe Jonas

Mentorship relationships don't always have to be formal relationships. Sometimes they can be as simple as "if I have a question, can I send you an email?" relationships. And these are great as well. While individually these relationships might not change your life drastically, having many of these kinds of mentors can make a big difference. So how can you increase this network of informal mentors?

Here are a few different ways to do it:

- If you run a business, talk to your lawyer and your accountant. Hire the best lawyers you can, even if you don't need their legal services yet. Why? And if your company can't afford their services yet, you can talk to the lawyer or accountant you consult with. Do it for the network. The best lawyers also have high level clients. Have them do the introductions for you.

- Another way you can make contact with successful individuals is through social networking. Many CEOs today run their own *Twitter feeds*. Retweeting their messages and @replying to them can help build a relationship so you can eventually drop them an email or ask for their emails.

- When the opportunities arise, attend conferences and trade shows. Meet influencers in person, build a connection and ask them to consider mentoring you – asking someone face to face makes a person stop and think about the request. For many it is a flattering request, especially when the request is asked by someone who is genuine and likeable.

The Authenticity Key

The key to making a great impression on a potential mentor is through authenticity. You have to be real and genuine. Imagine for a moment what the world is like from the eyes of the influential- a lot of people want your attention, but the vast majority of them want your attention so they can get something from you, or say they were with you or some often have an ulterior motive. And this is why successful people put up walls of resistance. The best way around these walls is to be genuine and authentic.

BENEFITS
OF **MENTORING**

By Mary Shaub

FOR THE MENTOR

1) Allows the mentor to "give back" — to both the organization and the mentee

2) Reminds the mentor how to listen actively rather than passively

3) Encourages the mentor to share knowledge, which helps increase the mentor's sense of self-worth

4) Strengthens the mentor's interpersonal relationship skills

5) Teaches the mentor about other areas/departments within the organization

6) Helps re-energize the mentor's career

7) Leads to more personal satisfaction on the mentor's behalf

FOR THE MENTEE

1) Increases the mentee's self-confidence

2) Helps the mentee learn to take better control of her career

3) Teaches the mentee how to speak up and be heard

4) Educates the mentee on how to accept feedback in important areas, such as communications, technical abilities, change management and leadership skills

5) Improves the mentee's interpersonal relationship skills

6) Provides an important networking contact for the mentee

7) Helps the mentee better understand the organization's culture and unspoken rules, both of which can be critical for success

SOURCE: MANAGEMENT-MENTORS.COM

"A lot of people have gone further than they thought they could because someone else thought they could."
~Zig Ziglar

"I've learned that people will forget what you said, people will forget what you did, but people will never forget how you made them feel."
—Maya Angelou

"We make a living by what we get — we make a life by what we give."
~Winston Churchill

"Tell me and I forget, teach me and I may remember, involve me and I learn."
~Benjamin Franklin

VALUABLE RESOURCE A good example of a formal mentoring effort is the MDRT's Mentoring Program, which is a free service for the organization's members. Worldwide there are more than 6,000 MDRT mentoring teams; about 1,600 of those are in the United States. In the 2013-2014 period, the mean total years of MDRT membership among U.S. mentors was more than 13 years for both men and women. RA

If you're nervous about meeting them, say so. If you're building a business and want their help, be upfront about it. If you really have no idea and are trying to figure things out, let them know. Don't pretend to be their friend with an ulterior motive; be 100% honest from the get-go or act like you are dope and it will be an honor for them to be involved with you. Actually, it is the other way round.

Asking for Informal Mentorship

Don't go overboard with your requests. Your requests for mentorship should be relatively straightforward and shouldn't require much of a commitment from your mentor.

Ask them if you can send them an email if you ever have a question on a specific topic. You can also ask if you could do a quick phone call with them. Find out your potential mentor's preferred mode of communication. And honor it.

Repeat this process again and again and you'll gradually amass quite a number of successful people in different arenas that you can contact if you ever get stuck in your business.

CHAPTER EIGHT

INVESTORS AS MENTORS

"A mentor is someone who sees more talent and ability within you, than you see in yourself, and helps bring it out of you." Bob Proctor

It could be so interesting and relaxing when you have an investor who can mentor you. What a great combo! That would mean he understands your business, your personality and is not just leaving you to go and get massive returns on his investment even if you are a newbie entrepreneur.

Warren Buffett started his investment road trip with a top tour guide! Imagine Warren Buffett as your investment quarterback, or Bill Gates, Mark Zuckerberg or even my humble self with the wealth of experience and results I have to show as your internet business mentors? Goals smashing, right? Yeah. That's what having a mentor is like! But, let's be candid here.

You probably will never get access to such high worth individual especially if you are still learning the ropes and will take way longer to find an investor and mentor in one person. There is a hack here though; invest in their books and get a return on your investment as progress.

Box 2: Mentor versus manager

MENTOR — FOCUS IS ON HELPING THE MENTEE	MANAGER — FOCUS IS ON GETTING THINGS DONE
Focuses on supporting longer-term development for current and future roles	Focuses on the completion of tasks and immediate deadlines
Helps the mentee reflect on his or her practice and make a self-assessment of competence in relation to the KSF outline or other competency framework	Assesses performance against standards and conducts appraisals
Helps the mentee to see development opportunities and identify learning needs for the PDP	Enables the worker to deliver and perform; identifies performance issues to inform learning needs for the PDP
Helps the mentee to set goals and to learn, develop and progress	Sets objectives and checks that these have been met
Helps the mentee to monitor his or her progress in relation to the KSF outline or other competency framework	Monitors performance to ensure quality

If you don't know the first thing about the stock market and how it works, be kind to yourself. Even Warren Buffett had to start somewhere. And if you're up for trying a book he loves, read "The Intelligent Investor" by Benjamin Graham. First published in 1949, Buffett calls it "the best book on investment ever written." Spend a little to buy it and many other internet investments related books to become a billionaire. How's that for a return on investment?

MENTORING

Mentoring is a one-to-one relationship between an experienced professional (mentor) who shares their knowledge, skills and experience with a less experienced professional (mentee) to assist in their career progression.

How the mentor helps:

- Career introductions
- Corporate understanding
- Problem solving
- Overcome hurdles
- Explore work methods
- Career planning

In the workplace, mentoring goes a long way:

96% of mentees are able to apply their learning directly to their careers

75% of executives say mentoring plays a key role in their careers

71% of Fortune 500 companies have a mentoring program

88% of businesses with a mentor program say having one is invaluable

| 0 | 10 | 20 | 30 | 40 | 50 | 60 | 70 | 80 | 90 | 100 |

And if you need capital as much as you need investment, you can look for someone who offers a complementary business to what your business is involved in. And approach them to mentor you and give you capital to work hand in hand with their company since your services or products are complementary.

For instance, if you want to start a Laundromat business, you can look for a cleaning production company and tell them to give you capital in the form of cleaning supplies to use for your business while you start paying 6 months- 1 year down the road when your business can stand on its own. You can also collect washing machines from 2-3 of your mentors and offer to do the laundry for their household free. You just have to be creative, be willing to work and think outside the box and you are sure to find good mentors.

CHAPTER NINE

NICHE MENTORS OR GENERAL MENTORS?

"We all carry the seeds of greatness within us, but we need an image as a point of focus in order that they may sprout."~ Epictetus

When most entrepreneurs search for mentors, they have a tendency to search for generic "enterprise mentors." People who will help inform them on their path to success. This is great because their business acumen can guide you on the principles of business in terms of cash flow, structure, operations and other essentials.

However, entrepreneurs usually overlook to search for a niche mentor in addition to general enterprise/business mentors. Often instances searching for area of interest mentors is best than looking for a common enterprise mentor.

What is a "Niche Mentor?

A niche mentor can also be called an area of interest mentor and is somebody who is aware of only one particular space of what you are promoting very, very effectively. For instance, if you are setting up a retail ecommerce web site, a general mentor (maybe in retail) can tell you of retail operations, cash flow, inventory management and the likes. That mentor will however not be able to tell you of drop shipping techniques, affiliate marketing, search engine marketing, which are ways to promote your site to get increased traffic, simply because your terrains are different.

BENEFITS
OF **MENTORING**

By Mary Shaub

FOR THE MENTOR

1) Allows the mentor to "give back" — to both the organization and the mentee

2) Reminds the mentor how to listen actively rather than passively

3) Encourages the mentor to share knowledge, which helps increase the mentor's sense of self-worth

4) Strengthens the mentor's interpersonal relationship skills

5) Teaches the mentor about other areas/ departments within the organization

6) Helps re-energize the mentor's career

7) Leads to more personal satisfaction on the mentor's behalf

FOR THE MENTEE

1) Increases the mentee's self-confidence

2) Helps the mentee learn to take better control of her career

3) Teaches the mentee how to speak up and be heard

4) Educates the mentee on how to accept feedback in important areas, such as communications, technical abilities, change management and leadership skills

5) Improves the mentee's interpersonal relationship skills

6) Provides an important networking contact for the mentee

7) Helps the mentee better understand the organization's culture and unspoken rules, both of which can be critical for success

SOURCE: MANAGEMENT-MENTORS.COM

"A lot of people have gone further than they thought they could because someone else thought they could."
~Zig Ziglar

"I've learned that people will forget what you said, people will forget what you did, but people will never forget how you made them feel."
~Maya Angelou

"We make a living by what we get — we make a life by what we give."
~Winston Churchill

"Tell me and I forget, teach me and I may remember, involve me and I learn."
~Benjamin Franklin

VALUABLE RESOURCE A good example of a formal mentoring effort is the MDRT's Mentoring Program, which is a free service for the organization's members. Worldwide there are more than 6,000 MDRT mentoring teams; about 1,600 of those are in the United States. In the 2013-2014 period, the mean total years of MDRT membership among U.S. mentors was more than 13 years for both men and women. RA

They can't even tell you what your employee qualities should look like, necessary skills to garner to stay afloat, preventing online fraud and what have you.

Having a niche mentor may not fully apply to all enterprise as some businesses can get by with just the general business knowledge especially if you already possess the core skill that the business largely depends on. But if you are going into an irregular business, it would be best to look for mentors in that business.

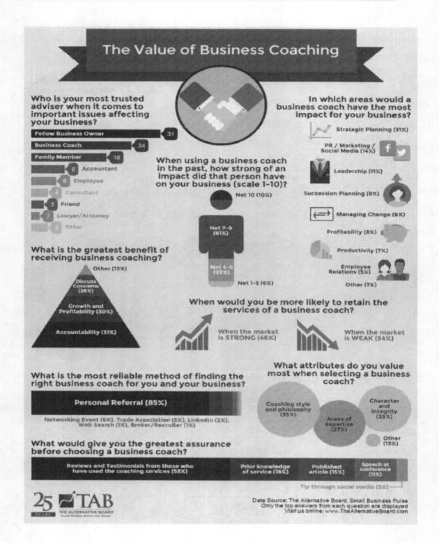

By and large, you need to figure out the areas you need mentoring by breaking down what you are trying to do or achieve by all of the completely different areas of experience wanted. To proceed with your e-commerce business for instance, the breakdown would possibly look one thing like this:

- Generating site visitors
- Running net software programs
- Finding wholesalers and distributors
- Ability to convert traffic into buyers

You could possibly search for mentors in every of those particular areas or for mentors in the e-commerce. It could be a little tricky trying to find mentors in that field as some may feel you are competitors. Some areas, like discovering wholesale traders, could be addressed by any mentor. Other areas, like discovering wholesalers from China to get cheaper deals, running technical programs, for instance, are addressed by specialists.

In some cases, you only get to meet with your mentor once a month or fortnightly which means you don't exactly have so much time with them. They also may not be able to reply your messages as urgently as you might want them to which is because they are busy too. Don't overlook employees who are skilled; they could be your mentors.

As Michael Dell says, your core group of workers ought to at all times be smarter than you. You should not be pulling your workers to the following stage; as an alternative they need to be pulling you. They should be on top of their game! You are the one with the vision but the vision needs so many skills which you might not necessarily possess. And it is fine. But your employees should be extremely good at the varied departments your company involves. Micromanaging people will kill you, leave you with less room to think, shape the idea and move your company to the next level.

CHAPTER TEN

APPROACHING A MENTOR

"What you want in a mentor is someone who truly cares for you and who will look after your interests and not just their own. When you do come across the right person to mentor you, start by showing them that the time they spend with you is worthwhile."
Vivek Wadhwa

Most people approach potential mentors in a completely wrong way. As a result, they find it extra challenging and difficult getting mentors to help them out. Stop approaching mentors with questions like "can we grab coffee sometime?", "will you mentor me?", "I'd really like to pick your brain". Those questions put potential mentors off.

Always remember when approaching mentors that they're also trying to get to the next level themselves. Sure, they might have a $10 million dollar company but they're also surrounded by people with $200 million dollar companies. They're trying to get their company to the next level as well as improve on themselves as well. There are a few things to keep in mind to set you apart from other people seeking their attention.

- Help them get to the next level.

If you help your mentors get to the next level, they'll naturally also want to help you get to the next level. If they are or their company get nominated for an award which requires voting, you could rally round votes for them. They might have a campaign and you could help them make more noise around it. Give value, get your hands dirty.

Guidelines for Approaching Mentors

- Do a self-Assessment and preparation of your CV

or biography sheet before meeting your mentor

- Preparation (become informed)
- Get an evaluation form that you can use to track what you are learning, actions you carried out and results

- Know their specific career path so that you don't start asking unrelated questions
- Ask questions relating to your current situation and future goals not questions like "how do you balance work-life?"

Other Tips for Approaching a Mentor

1. Do your homework on yourself

Be clear on what you want. Are you asking for in-depth career help, simple advice, or for some innovative ideas? After asking yourself these questions, it's OK to realize that perhaps part of what you need from a mentor is clarity on your next steps.

Getting clear about what you need—or at least understanding that you have no idea what you need—will help you frame your request for help.

2. Do your homework on the field

Take your time before you take their time. What information can you mine on the web about the sector you hope to enter, or the job you hope to obtain?

3. Do your homework on your potential mentor

Visit their website, if they have one, look at their LinkedIn profile and read any materials they may have published.

Get to know the person whose help you want before approaching them.

Sometimes ago, a chartered accountant, decided he wanted to become a business coach, he spent weeks researching the market before approaching me to ask for mentoring. During our meeting, he shared his analysis of a few ways he could enter the market and asked me for ideas of how else he could start to engage clients. He had studied my client list and came armed with specific questions. Because he did all three parts of his homework, I was more motivated to help him. He made efficient use of our time together and walked away with specific tips, action items, and contacts.

Make sure to follow these three guidelines when you "make the ask."

4. Value their time

The easiest way to show that you value your potential mentor's time is to approach them via a succinct email. Most people will immediately deal with emails that require less than a minute to process and ignore more complicated messages. Here's an example of a well-executed "ask" email:

Subject: 15 mins of your time - your expertise in healthcare
Dear Mentor,

In 10 years, I aspire to be where you are in your career today: coaching executives and working with leadership teams in the healthcare sector. Based on the testimonials on your website, your methodology has clearly made a big impact.

I'd appreciate your help to understand how you entered the healthcare market so I might begin a similar career path.
One of my friends really admires your skills and suggested I get in touch with you. Your insights will add something I can't glean from the research I've done on this sector.

I know your time is precious, so I'd like to limit my request to 15 minutes of your time at your convenience. I promise to keep our conversation brief, as I've already done homework on the field and your work. Also, if there's anything I can do to help return the favor, please let me know.
Thanks in advance,
Mentee

5. Be accommodating

When asking someone for help, make it easy for them to help you! Remember, you are asking for a favor, so you need to accommodate their schedule and make it easy for them to say yes.

For instance, someone asked me for help on how to become a coach. At that time, I was immersed in day-long training sessions, business meetings on Saturdays and offered to speak to her on Sunday. She replied: "Sundays are used for my religious activities and my family, so can you talk during the week?" While I admired her for setting a clear boundary around family and religion time, I wasn't able to accommodate her request. She wanted my help but was inflexible about when to receive it.

6. Keep it short

People who ask for 15 minutes of someone's time are more likely to get on that person's calendar than those who ask for an hour. This is also an indication you respect the mentor's time.

7. State what you want up front

Rapport building is important, but don't spend the first 20 minutes on small talk like you are buddies. Tell them up front what you'd like. Skipping the small talk may feel uncomfortable but starting with a polite introduction and then jumping into business is the best way to stay on track.

8. Ask what you can do for the mentor

Most mentors choose to help people purely to give back, but it never hurts to ask what favors you can provide in return for their help. When people ask what they can do for me, I ask them to comment on or share my articles. The few people who follow through on this request stand out and I feel more inclined to give them more of my time.

9. Thank your mentor

This may seem like a no-brainer, but about a quarter of the people I mentor never send follow-up thank you emails. Again, most mentors don't help others to be thanked, but common courtesy helps. Besides, a thank you email offers another communication touchpoint with your mentor. Emails are an integral part of building a lasting, mutually-beneficial relationship; remember to send regular emails telling your mentor how her advice has helped you.

10. Make Sure You're Asking the Right Person

Choosing the right person as a mentor is probably the biggest factor to whether they'll accept your request. Most people want mentors who exemplify their vision of success—business leaders, entrepreneurs, recognizable names—it's easy to want to have a famous businessperson, developer, or activist as your personal mentor. Odds are though, those people are already busy or unavailable, and while it never hurts to ask, the odds are heavily against you. Remember, your mentor doesn't have to be a household name to be a good one—anyone whose experience and wisdom you can learn from would make a great mentor.

*When you're looking for someone to be your mentor, look for people who have the title, position, or experience you're trying to get. Don't set your sights too far off into the future. Think about your next few career goals and look for people who match, preferably people you know personally or could easily meet. If your company has a mentorship program, start there. Participants are looking for people to mentor, so you'll have an easier time finding someone willing to take you under their wing. If not, consider a manager in your own department, or another department in your company that you work closely with. Ask a friend or someone in your professional network to connect you with someone in their company who's willing to take on a mentor and has the position you're looking for.

*Whoever you choose, pick someone you can get some personal contact with, or can easily meet and talk to face to face. It may seem like a good idea to aim high and ask someone you've never met (but whose work you're familiar with) to be your mentor, but you'll have better luck asking someone with whom you already have a personal connection. A far off face on the Internet may be able to trade emails with you from time to time, but they likely won't be able to pay individual, regular attention to you. Someone who's personally invested in your success and can check in with you regularly when you need advice—or when you have a question—is a much better pick.

11. Ask The Right Way

When you do ask someone to be your mentor, keep in mind that you're asking them for a favor—one that will likely require a good bit of energy on their part. You're not paying them for their time, and they don't owe you anything. If they're part of a mentoring program or have been a mentor in the past, they likely know this already, but even so, approach the question with the appropriate care, empathy, and lack of self-entitlement. The fastest way to get the old "Sorry, I don't have time right now" response is to overconfidently demand your prospective mentor's time and attention.

12.   Come to the table with how much time and attention you think you'll need.

Don't make them guess how much of a time sink you'll be. Let them know up front how much time and attention you really think your mentor/mentee relationship will demand. Remember, your prospective mentor is likely busy with their own projects.

13.   Be ready to explain what you want to get out of the mentorship, why you want the person you're asking to be your mentor, and why you want a mentor in the first place. You don't have to stroke the other person's ego, but you should explain that you know who they are and you value their expertise. Let them know that their career mirrors your would-be career path, and you think you could learn a lot from them. If you can, share a story they would resonate with—or a story of theirs you already know and what you learned from it.

14.   Make your case based on common experiences and interests.
Remember, getting a mentor to work with you is less of a job interview and more of a friend request. If you feel like their angle is "well, what do I get out of this," you may want to back off, but do let them know that you feel like you may be able to learn from each other if they'll give you a chance. If you do have common interests or hobbies, play that up too.

15.   Explain you're looking for advice and guidance, not a tutor.

Your mentor shouldn't do your work for you, and they should know from the outset that you're looking to learn from their experience—not have them essentially be the parent you ask for help every time you're stuck with your homework.

16.   If your question seems to make your prospective mentor uncomfortable, back off.

Mentors, like references, should be 100% dedicated to the task of helping you out. If you get the vibe that they feel pressured or don't really want to be in the position you're putting them in, let them out—if you force them into it, you won't get the best possible experience anyway, and worse, you may be imposing.

17.   Know When to Follow Up (and When Not To

Like we mentioned earlier, your mentor should be engaged—not just with the idea of mentoring, but with mentoring you specifically. If you ask them to be your mentor and then offer to follow up later, follow up to see how they're feeling about it. if they waffle, or they give you anything less than a confident answer, then let it go and look for someone else. You're not going to get the best time and attention from someone who's going to be annoyed every time you ask them out for coffee, or who felt pressured into being your mentor. If you ever start to get that vibe from your mentor, it's time to let them off the hook, thank them for everything they've taught you up to that point, and offer to stay in touch.

If they're amenable to the idea, it's time to seal the deal and give them an idea of how often you'll connect with them and when you'll get in touch. They may take the lead, but don't expect them to. You can take a load off of their plate by mapping out when you should talk and how you'll be in touch, especially if you just need advice from time to time. Whatever you agree to, make sure you follow up, meet when you say you're going to, and drop them a line from time to time just to check in. If there's ever a doubt, take the initiative. Remember, you're there to learn and soak up as much as possible from *them*. Don't make them work just to get a hold of you.

18.   Keep Your Relationship Strong, and Pay It Forward

Once you've landed a great mentor, do what it takes to keep that relationship strong. Not only do you have someone you can learn from, but you'll have someone valuable in your professional network who can help you when the chips are down, or you can offer a hand to when you have something to offer. When they give you advice, make sure you take it, and when you're not sure what you should talk about, ask them what you should be asking them.

Mentoring happens every day in the business world. Sometimes, you're lucky enough to get unbidden mentoring. But, mostly, you have to ask to receive. When asking a potential mentor for help, approaching that person with intention, intelligence and gratitude makes all the difference between a 'no' and a 'yes'. The more you can make a complete case for what you're looking for, why you chose them, and how much of an investment you represent, the easier it'll be for your potential mentor to say yes.

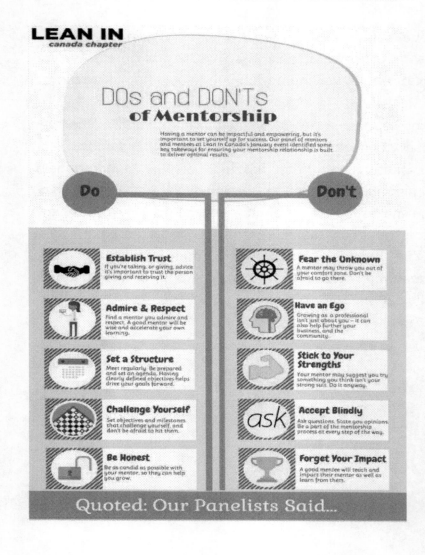

DOs and DON'Ts of Mentorship

Having a mentor can be impactful and empowering, but it's important to set yourself up for success. Our panel of mentors and mentees at Lean In Canada's January event identified some key takeways for ensuring your mentorship relationship is built to deliver optimal results.

Do

Establish Trust
If you're taking, or giving, advice it's important to trust the person giving and receiving it.

Admire & Respect
Find a mentor you admire and respect. A good mentor will be wise and accelerate your own learning.

Set a Structure
Meet regularly. Be prepared and set an agenda. Having clearly defined objectives helps drive your goals forward.

Challenge Yourself
Set objectives and milestones that challenge yourself, and don't be afraid to hit them.

Be Honest
Be as candid as possible with your mentor, so they can help you grow.

Don't

Fear the Unknown
A mentor may throw you out of your comfort zone. Don't be afraid to go there.

Have an Ego
Growing as a professional isn't just about you – it can also help further your business, and the community.

Stick to Your Strengths
Your mentor may suggest you try something you think isn't your strong suit. Do it anyway.

Accept Blindly
Ask questions. State you opinions. Be a part of the mentorship process at every step of the way.

Forget Your Impact
A good mentee will teach and impact their mentor as well as learn from them.

Quoted: Our Panelists Said...

What Not to Do?

1. Asking for the Mentor Upfront

Would you ask someone to be your spouse on the first date? Not likely. Being so abrupt is a bad idea on a first date, and you should treat your first encounter with a mentor the same way. There isn't enough time or information in one meeting to predict if a mentorship bond exists between you. Your best bet is to ask for the meeting; not the mentorship. Most people will grant you a 15-minute conversation to answer any specific questions. Here's a line that always works: "I enjoyed our conversation. Should a specific question arise, would it be okay if I reached out for a 15-minute chat to continue the conversation?"

2. Not Establishing Rules for Following Up

You get one chance to make an impression on a potential mentor. Use this time to set up an agreement for your next encounter.

I usually say, 'I'm going to send you an update email in three weeks after I work on the strategy we talked about.'" They could, of course, say "no thanks,". But usually, when you set expectations upfront, if you send a message, they will refer back to the email chain and honor the request.

3. Chasing Names Over Relevant Experience

A participant in my mentoring workshop was adamant she could never find her ideal mentor. So, I started by asking her what she wanted to do. She told me that she wanted to start local food business. "And who is your ideal mentor?" I asked. "The CEO of Mr. Biggs." She had, like so many, made the mistake of chasing a name over experience. The CEO of Mr. Biggs has no idea how to help her; he hasn't opened a small food shop in years. A more relevant mentor is the restaurant owner one town over, who opened a shop two years ago. Make sure you can explain to your mentor-to-be how their experience relates to what you want to do.

4. Replying "None of Those Times Work"

David Simnick, the founder of Soapbox, a socially conscious soap company with explosive growth, gets approached to be a mentor quite often. His pet peeve is an inflexible mentee. "When you are reaching out to someone with experience and knowledge, who can save you years of mistake and heartache, the most insulting thing you can do is care about your own calendar. Please don't reply 'none of those times work,'" he says. "You are reaching out to me and, as a courtesy, should demonstrate an effort to work around my schedule."

5. Asking Questions You Can Easily Google

What do you think would happen if you asked Larry Page, the founder of Google, how to start a flower business in college? He would probably tell you to Google it, and with good reason: At this level, he is more likely engaged by questions about the future of cloud computing and Google's telecom play— questions he is uniquely qualified to answer.

6. Making It All About You

The idea that some Dumbledore-like mentor will imbue a young Harry Potter with all the knowledge he needs to succeed is untrue. The truth is, in today's noisy competition for mentors, two-way relationships are the most likely to succeed. One of the mentors who attended my trainings gushed at how much value she got from her mentee, telling us: "What I loved most about Simone is that she always asked me how she could help me, volunteered to help at nonprofit events, and even played the role of my confidant from time-to-time. These experiences and her willingness to give deepened our relationship immensely."

7. Not Expressing Gratitude

Never underestimate the power of gratitude in a mentor relationship. Updated emails tracking your progress and expressing genuine appreciation for your mentors' help goes a long way.

Functions/Roles of Mentors

The following are among the mentor's functions:

- Teaches the mentee about a specific issue
- Coaches the mentee on a particular skill
- Facilitates the mentee's growth by sharing resources and networks
- Challenges the mentee to move beyond his or her comfort zone
- Creates a safe learning environment for taking risks
- Focuses on the mentee's total development
- A mentor takes a long-range view on your growth and development.
- A mentor helps you see the destination but does not give you the detailed map to get there.
- A mentor offers encouragement and cheerleading, but not "how to" advice.

What a Mentor Does Not Do for You:

- A mentor is not a coach as explained above.
- A mentor is typically not an advocate of yours in the organizational environment: the relationship is private.

- A mentor is not going to tell you how to do things.
- A mentor is not there to support you on transactional, short-term problems.
- A mentor is not a counselor.

Ideas to Help You Succeed With a Mentor:

Understanding the role of the mentor is a critical starting point for success in this relationship. Additional requirements include:

1. Investing your time in seeking out the mentor.
2. Sharing your goals and fears openly.
3. Not expecting the mentor to solve your short-term problems or do the work for you.
4. Not expecting specific advice.
5. Sharing where you are struggling or failing.
6. Listening carefully and then researching and applying the mentor's guidance.
7. Showing that you value the mentor's support.
8. Not abusing the relationship by expecting political support in the organization.

CHAPTER ELEVEN

MENTORING AND COACHING

"One who refuses to seek the advice of others will eventually be led to a path of ruin. A mentor helps you to perceive your own weaknesses and confront them with courage. The bond between mentor and protege enables us to stay true to our chosen path until the very end."

A lot of people confuse mentoring with coaching and vice-versa. We have seen the definition of mentoring above and what the mentoring relationship entails. Now, are

mentoring and coaching identical twins? No.

The terms mentoring and coaching are often used interchangeably, and that is misleading. While similar in their support of someone's development, they are very different disciplines in practice.

Mentoring is a long-term relationship where the focus is on supporting the growth and development of the mentee. The mentor is a source of wisdom, teaching, and support, but not someone who observes and advises on specific actions or behavioral changes in daily work.

Coaching is typically a relationship of finite duration where the focus is on strengthening or eliminating specific behaviors in the here and now.

Coaches are engaged to help professionals correct behaviors that detract from their performance or, to strengthen those that support stronger performance around a set of activities.

Both mentoring and coaching are incredibly valuable in providing developmental support.

However, one offers high-level guidance for the long-term development, and the other helps you improve immediately.

"More than mere teachers, mentors are often emancipators, freeing artists from poor technique, clouded vision and personal uncertainty." -Paul Soderberg

Though related, they are not the same. A mentor may coach, but a coach is not a mentor. Mentoring is "relational," while coaching is "functional." There are other significant differences. And I have highlighted some of the different characteristics across the two.

Coaching Characteristics

- Managers coach all of their staff as a required part of the job
- Coaching takes place within the confines of a formal manager-employee relationship
- Focuses on developing individuals within their current jobs
- Interest is functional, arising out of the need to ensure that individuals can perform the tasks required to the best of their abilities
- Relationship tends to be initiated and driven by an individual's manager
- Relationship is finite - ends as individual transfers to another job

Mentoring Characteristics

- Takes place outside of a line manager-employee relationship, at the mutual consent of a mentor and the person being mentored
- Is career-focused or focuses on professional development that may be outside a mentor's area of work
- Relationship is personal - a mentor provides both professional and personal support

Relationship may be initiated by a mentor or created through a match initiated by the organization

- Relationship crosses job boundaries
- Relationship may last for a specific period of time (nine months to a year) in a formal program, at which point the pair may continue in an informal mentoring relationship

CHAPTER TWELVE

FREQUENTLY ASKED QUESTIONS

"No man is capable of self-iprovement if he sees no other model but himself." -Conrado I. Generoso

Are buddy systems and mentoring programs the same?

No. Buddy systems are initiated by organizations to help new employees adjust to jobs during their first few months of employment.

Buddies are most often peers in the same department, who assist new employees for short periods of time and require no specialized training as a buddy.

Mentoring is a more complex relationship and focuses on both short- and long-term professional development goals. Though a mentor may be an employee's peer, most often a mentor is a person at least one level higher in the organization who is not within the mentee's direct supervisory line of management.

> "If your mentors only that you are awesome, it's time to find other mentors."- Cosette Gutierrez

Organizations formal mentoring programs?

Interest in mentoring has varied over time and has been affected by economic and social factors.

Organizations recognize that workforce demographics have changed dramatically in recent years, as women and members of different minority groups have joined the workforce in greater numbers.

In addition, technology has automated traditional employee functions and continues to affect on-the-job performance, altering the way people see themselves within the corporate structure.

With these changes, organizations are finding it difficult to recruit and retain qualified personnel. As corporate downsizing continues, organizations are also experiencing a flattening of their organizations, challenging them to provide sufficient growth opportunities for employees.

On the plus side, organizations find today's employees exhibit a more flexible approach to work. On the minus side, employees may feel less loyalty to the organizations for which they work.

Organizations now look to mentoring to implement a strategic game plan that includes:

Recruitment
Retention
Professional development
Development of a multicultural workforce

Does mentoring happen naturally?

Absolutely. Informal mentoring occurs all the time and is a powerful experience. The problem is that informal mentoring is often accessible only to a few people or employees (in organizational mentoring) and its benefits are limited only to those few who participate. Formal or structured mentoring takes mentoring to the next level and expands its usefulness and corporate value beyond that of a single mentor-mentee pairing.

How are informal and formal mentoring different?

Informal and formal mentoring are often confused, but they are very different in their approaches and outcomes.

Informal mentoring:

- Goals of the relationship are not specified
- Outcomes are not measured
- Access is limited and may be exclusive
- Mentors and mentees self-select on the basis of personal chemistry
- Mentoring lasts a long time; sometimes a lifetime
- The organization benefits indirectly, as the focus is exclusively on the mentee

Formal mentoring

- Goals are established from the beginning by the organization and the employee mentored
- Outcomes are measured
- Access is open to all who meet program criteria
- Mentors and mentorees are paired based on compatibility
- Training and support in mentoring is provided Organization and employee both benefits directly.

What is "chemistry" and "compatibility?"

"Chemistry" is an intense, very personal feeling – an initial connection or attraction between two individuals that may develop into a strong, emotional bond. Unstructured and unpredictable, it is the basis for an informal mentoring relationship.

"Compatibility" occurs when individuals work together in harmony to achieve a common purpose. In formal mentoring, that means a more-seasoned person leading someone less experienced through a structured professional-development program in much the same way teachers facilitate learning.

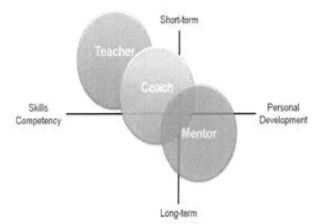

Why do

organizations need a structured mentoring program?

Many people do not see the essence of an organizational mentoring program because they feel managers are

already performing the role? While many managers try to demonstrate mentoring behavior on an informal basis, it is very different from having a structured mentoring program.

There is a qualitative difference between a manager-employee relationship and a mentor-mentee relationship. More so, the manager has a duty to oversee the duties of the junior employee and make sure the deliverable and KPI's are met. Merging the two together might not work so well.

- **Managerial Role**

The manager-employee relationship focuses on achieving the objectives of the department and the company. The manager assigns tasks, evaluates the outcome, conducts performance reviews, and recommends possible salary increases and promotions.

Because managers hold significant power over employees' work lives, most employees demonstrate only their strengths and hide their weaknesses in the work environment.

- **Mentoring Role**

A mentor-mentee relationship focuses on developing the mentee professionally and personally. As such, the mentor does not evaluate the mentee with respect to his or her current job, does not conduct performance reviews of the mentee, and does not provide input about salary increases and promotions.

This creates a safe learning environment, where the mentee feels free to discuss issues openly and honestly, without worrying about negative consequences on the job.

The roles of manager and mentor are fundamentally different. That's why structured mentoring programs never pair mentors with their direct reports.

Organizational **benefits** **of** mentoring?
Mentoring benefits the organization, mentors and mentees. A successful mentoring program benefits your organization by:
- Enhancing strategic business initiatives
- Encouraging retention
- Reducing turnover costs
- Improving productivity
- Breaking down the "silo" mentality that hinders

" Your mentor does not need to be exactly like you to give good advice; he or she just needs to understand your situation. "

cooperation among company departments or divisions.

- Elevating knowledge transfer from just getting information and to retaining the practical experience and wisdom gained from long-term employees.
- Enhancing professional development.
- Linking employees with valuable knowledge and information to other employees in need of such information
- Using your own employees, instead of outside consultants, as internal experts for professional development
- Supporting the creation of a multicultural workforce by creating relationships among diverse employees and allowing equal access to mentoring.
- Creating a mentoring culture, which continuously promotes individual employee growth and development.

Mentors enjoy many benefits, including:
- Gains insights from the mentee's background and history that can be used in the mentor's professional and personal development.
- Gains satisfaction in sharing expertise with others.
- Re-energizes the mentor's career.

- Gains an ally in promoting the organization's well-being.
- Learns more about other areas within the organization.

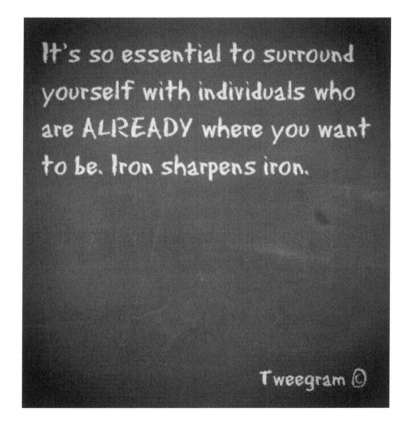

It's so essential to surround yourself with individuals who are ALREADY where you want to be. Iron sharpens iron.

Tweegram ©

Mentees enjoy many benefits, including:
- Gains from the mentor's expertise

- Receives critical feedback in key areas, such as communications, interpersonal relationships, technical abilities, change management and leadership skills
- Develops a sharper focus on what is needed to grow professionally within the organization
- Learns specific skills and knowledge that are relevant to personal goals
- Networks with a more influential employee
- Gains knowledge about the organization's culture and unspoken rules that can be critical for success; as a result, adapts more quickly to the organization's culture
- Has a friendly ear with which to share frustrations as well as successes?

How does an organization know when it's ready to implement a formal mentoring program?

An organization that values its employees and is committed to providing opportunities for them to remain and grow within the organization is an ideal candidate for initiating a mentoring program. Ideally, the organization has an internal structure to support a successful program.

Examples include:
- A performance management program
- Developed competencies
- A valued-training function
- Diversity training
- A succession-planning process
- A management development program
- Strategic business objectives

In addition, there should be individuals within the higher ranks of the organization who will champion the mentoring initiative and help make it happen. Advocates may include the organization's president, vice presidents and other influential executives.

A Mentoring Program Manager (MPM) is also needed to coordinate the mentoring program. The MPM should be someone who is perceived as a facilitator, listener and coalition-builder – a person who is trusted. MPM is not a

---

"Mentoring brings us together- across generation, class, and often race- in a manner that forces us to acknowledge our interdependence, to appreciate, in Martin Luther King, Jr.'s words, that 'we are caught in an inescapable network of mutuality, tied in a single garment of destiny.' In this way, mentoring enables us to participate in the essential but unfinished drama of reinventing community, while reaffirming that there is an important role for each of us in it."

Marc Freedman

---

full-time position, so mentoring responsibilities must be balanced with the MPM's other duties. Typically, such a person works in a Human Resources, Organizational

What does a Mentoring Program Manager do?

Coordinating the mentoring process within the organization means working with a Management Mentors consultant, as well as fellow employees, to design and implement a mentoring initiative that fits the organization's culture.

The initiative forms the basis for ongoing mentoring. During the pilot, a Mentoring Program Manager (MPM) typically works with 20 to 30 individuals (10 to 15 pairs). The manager contacts them on a regular basis, making certain the relationships are going well and that the mentoring program is achieving its goals. The MPM offers each pair whatever resources may be needed. The MPM also becomes the organization's internal mentoring expert, serving as a resource for various departments and divisions that have an interest in pursuing mentoring.

The amount of time this take varies. Normally, a MPM spends one to four hours per week coordinating the project, depending on how often the mentor-mentee pairs meet.

"SO MANY ORGANIZATIONS HAVE A MENTORING ARM, BUT THEY DON'T REALLY DO IT. THEIR IDEA OF MENTORING A KID IS GIVING THEM GENERAL ADVICE. BUT WHAT THEY NEED DO IS READ WITH THE CHILDREN." -WALTER DEAN

How can we create a pilot mentoring program?

The Mentoring Program Manager forms a task force of 6-8 people. Members of the task force should represent a cross-section of the organization, including potential mentors and mentees, supervisory personnel and any stakeholders who can bring value to the process. For example, a representative from Human Resources might help tie department goals with the goals of the mentoring program.

The task force:
- Determines the goals of the program
- Chooses the proper mentoring model
- Selects criteria for mentors and mentees
- Defines other critical components of the program
- Interviews potential candidates
- Matches participants
- Evaluates results at the end of the pilot program

How can you determine an organization's need for mentoring?

Some organizations conduct focus groups, employee surveys or both to determine where the need for mentoring is greatest, and whether there is sufficient support for a mentoring program.

Other organizations rely on task force members, who have been asked to participate because of their knowledge of the organization and the population being targeted. The appropriate method depends on what steps an organization has already taken as well as what resources are available.

Are there different types of mentoring models in a structured program?

One of the advantages of mentoring is that it can be adapted to any organization's culture and resources. There are several mentoring models to choose from when developing a mentoring program, including:

- ### *One-On-One* *Mentoring*

The most common mentoring model, one-on-one mentoring matches one mentor with one mentee. Most people prefer this model because it allows both mentor and mentee to develop a personal relationship and provides individual support for the mentee. Availability of mentors is the only limitation.

- ### *Resource-Based* *Mentoring*

Resource-based mentoring offers some of the same features as one-on-one mentoring. The main difference is that mentors and mentees are not interviewed and matched by a Mentoring Program Manager. Instead, mentors agree to add their names to a list of available mentors from which a mentee can choose. It is up to the mentee to initiate the process by asking one of the volunteer mentors for assistance. This model typically has limited support within the organization and may result in mismatched mentor-mentee pairing.

- *Group* *Mentoring*

Group mentoring requires a mentor to work with 4-6 mentees at one time. The group meets once or twice a month to discuss various topics. Combining senior and peer mentoring, the mentor and the peers help one another learn and develop

appropriate skills and knowledge. Group mentoring is limited by the difficulty of regularly scheduling meetings for the entire group. It also lacks the personal relationship that most people prefer in mentoring. For this reason, it is often combined with the one-on-one model. For example, some organizations provide each mentee with a specific mentor. In addition, the organization offers periodic meetings in which a senior executive meets with all of the mentors and mentees, who then share their knowledge and expertise.

- **_Training-Based_**   _Mentoring_

This model is tied directly to a training program. A mentor is assigned to a mentee to help that person develop the specific skills being taught in the program. Training-based mentoring is limited, because it focuses on the subject at hand and doesn't help the mentee develop a broader skill set.

- **_Executive_**   _Mentoring_

This top-down model may be the most effective way to create a mentoring culture and cultivate skills and knowledge throughout an organization. It is also an effective succession-planning tool, because it prevents the knowledge "brain drain" that would otherwise take place when senior management retires.

What   is the role of diversity in mentoring?

Mentoring can be of great value to women and people of color. These are the employees who have often been disenfranchised within organizations and have not been

"chosen"   by   informal   mentors.

However, if mentoring is to be successful as a tool for empowering employees, it needs to be truly diverse – representing everyone within the organization and not just women and people of color. By including the broadest spectrum of people, mentoring offers everyone the opportunity to grow professionally and personally without regard to gender or race. A successful mentoring program needs to balance the need for inclusion with the need for fair representation.

For many years, some organizations thought of mentoring only as a tool to help women and people of color. Viewed inappropriately as a remedial program, mentoring lacked widespread support within most organizations.

These mentoring programs did not provide mentees with the assistance they really needed. Good intentions gone astray resulted in a misapplication of mentoring.

Diversity is equally important when choosing mentors within organizations. Because many mentoring programs are geared to management levels, today's mentor population still tends to be made up of white males.

As organizations seek to devise mentoring programs, they need to include mentors who are both non-white and non-male. Using the resource-based or group-based models, tied to the one-on-one mentoring model, can help diversify   the   mentor   population.

For example, one of the mentoring goals might be to learn how to navigate effectively through the organization's culture. Using the group model, an organization might have a panel of diverse employees meeting with the entire mentor-mentee population to share how they have successfully navigated that culture.

What results can be achieved in a structured mentoring program?

Though a great deal has been written about mentoring, there is little statistical data supporting its value. Much of the published information available is based on theory alone. Because mentoring is about human relationships, it is more difficult to quantify scientifically.

Using interviews and questionnaires, Management Mentors has evaluated mentoring programs implemented by client companies. The results consistently demonstrate that well-designed programs lead to the acquisition of knowledge and expertise within a trusting and supportive mentoring relationship.

Why can't we create a program ourselves?

Creating a structured mentoring program requires a solid

understanding of mentoring dynamics. There are myriad examples of mentoring programs that failed because organizations mistakenly believed they fully understood mentoring. Rather than create a successful program, they negatively impacted the careers of both mentors and mentees. Typically, such programs have put people together without clear guidelines, offered no training about mentoring relationships, lacked internal support, paired employees with the bosses of the employees' immediate supervisors, and violated other fundamentals of mentoring. The amount of outside expertise needed to establish a mentoring program varies from organization to organization. Most organizations have found that using a consultant to set up a pilot program has made the difference between success and failure.

The Bottom Line

A mentor can be a difference maker in your career and life. It is important to come to the relationship with open eyes on the role and to have proper expectations. And remember, the impact of a mentor's guidance and wisdom now may not be felt for years to come. However, it will be felt.

https://www.forbes.com/sites/georgedeeb/2014/08/28 /is-a-startup-incubator-or-accelerator-right-for-you/?s=trending#6b8c0c243d7a

http://www.chrisjsnook.com/my-rants/2015/2/12/clear-distinctions-mentor-v-board-advisor-v-board-director

https://www.thebalance.com/how-to-make-a-mint-with-an-

Stephen Akintayo, (Africa Most Sought-after Investment Coach) an inspirational speaker and Serial Entrepreneur is currently the Chief Executive Officer of Stephen Akintayo Consulting International and Gtext Media and Investment Limited, a leading firm in Nigeria whose services span from Digital Marketing, Website Design, Bulk SMS, Online Advertising, Media, E-Commerce, Real Estate, Consulting and a host of other services.

Stephen, Also Founded GileadBalm Group Services which has assisted a number of businesses in Nigeria to move to enviable levels by helping them reach their clients through its enormous nationwide data base of real phone numbers and email addresses. It has hundreds of organizations as its clients including multinational companies like Guarantee Trust Bank, PZ Cussons, MTN, Chivita, among others.

Stephen, popularly called Pastor Stephen is also the founder of Omonaija, an online radio station and SAtv in Lagos currently streaming for 24 hours daily with the capacity to reach every country of the world.

To invite **Stephen Akintayo** for a speaking engagement kindly visit stephenakintayo.com email: info@stephenakintayo.com or call: 08180000618

Made in the USA
Columbia, SC
23 April 2024

34403037R10100